Google Advertising Advanced Search Exam Prep Guide for AdWords Certification
Version 1.2 / 2014 Edition

Keith Penn

Published in the United States
Version 1.2

Praise for the SearchCerts.com Exam Prep Series

"Explains all angles of the certification, from benefits to the way Google handles its partners." - Andrew Kobylarz, Account Executive

"Talking about the 'things to look out for' while answering questions and just general question strategy I feel is helpful, and reminds me of the strong test preps I did for my GMAT." - Jordan Bell, Marketing Manager

"Bottom line: Get this book if you have some basic hands-on knowledge of AdWords and you are looking to pass the AdWords test and join the Google Partner Program." - Elie Orgel, SEO Director

About the Author

I research and publish exam prep materials for the certifications and exams of the Google Analytics Individual Qualification (GAIQ), both Search and Display AdWords certifications, and Bing's Accreditation. I personally hold these and renew more often than necessary. My advertising and sales background is wide across search, display, spot TV, events, and print. The nuts and bolts of how those work are different, but they serve the same purpose. Earlier experience includes news production and military service, and I hold an MA and BA, both in communication from public universities in my native Texas. All this makes me unusual in the halls of many companies and gives me a big advantage when it comes to conveying what I learn to others. These days I live in Queens, NY where distance running is even harder to pursue. My day job finds me researching and evaluating digital advertising practices. - Keith Penn

Acknowledgements

Thanks to Karina for keeping me on topic and on time. Thanks to those whose brains I've picked, both on the Google Certification Program team and those who shared their exam experiences. You've made this a better guide than I could have composed on my own. Thanks to the performance marketing professionals who reviewed beta drafts and found wrongs in need of righting. Some things can only be seen through a reader's eyes and this work wouldn't be as useful without your shaping and sharpening of each revision. - Keith Penn

Contents

PART I: PREPARING FOR THE EXAM

This is one of a series of AdWords certification guides, which each share the exact same Part I covering the Google Partners Program certifications and specifics about tactics for passing the AdWords exams on the first try. If you've previously read another guide in this series and remember it well, then you might skip right ahead to Part II which exclusively covers the exam this guide is for. All material is updated as often as necessary to keep up with the changes to the Google Partners Program, certifications, and tests.

CHAPTER 1: What & Who this Guide is For

In the minds of many people, Google is the only pay-per-click advertising company that exists. There are others, but Google is the standard in performance marketing and if you want to show some credibility in the field, then you want their certification.

The furthest back I can trace the birth of this guide is to a time I was trying to impress a client over the phone while working at a company that provided incremental search traffic. He was a Director of Search Engine Marketing and oversaw an AdWords budget in excess of $100,000 per month, and spending substantially less than that with me. I told him I spent lunch studying-up for the Fundamentals Exam and was going to take it that weekend.

He joked we should be "coffee shop study buddies" (though he and I live in different cities) because he failed it recently and was planning to retest soon. He said his entire AdWords budget went to text search ads, while half the test is about products he never buys and features that serve no purpose for him. The realization that he and I were both learning about some of the same things for the first time certainly woke me up.

It took a lot more than a week before I took (and passed) the test the first time. Most of that time was spent googling topics, favoriting video tutorials, trudging through how-to blog posts, and bookmarking so many pages that bookmark management became a hassle.

Google's stated mission "to organize the world's information" is not evident in their Learning Center. It covers so much material that could never be on the test. Subjects like airport targeting and detailed instructions begin with a warning that they're meant for programmers only - and not people taking AdWords exams. I found myself thinking I would gladly pay money if the material I needed to know for the exam (and nothing else) could all be spelled-out so the time it would take to get certified could be shortened. I wanted an exam prep guide.

How Far will Experience Take Me?

Experience counts and it'll take you farther than any other single factor. Relying on experience also means you did this the hard way. Clever Kevin (who's brand new) may study harder than you this month, but he could get the same score you'll get (with your years of experience) by answering the same number of questions correctly. Of course if you *are* a Clever Kevin, then realize that no amount of midnight oil will replace years of familiarization.

Many questions and answers on the tests are outdated, which favors those who know through experience. The AdWords platform evolves and exams of proficiency evolve a little more slowly. This is one way experience can trump book knowledge, even in academic-smelling standardized testing. If a question asks about a feature that was discontinued last year, how would someone who learned AdWords this year be expected to know the answer? When an obsolete question that hasn't yet been scrubbed from the test is presented, the person who knows the obsolete answer is the one who remembers it through experience.

If it's on the test, then it's in this guide. Every question that I've ever seen on the real test can be answered with the material of Part II. You'll notice questions and answers that don't apply in a post-Enhanced Campaigns world *only if* they're still showing up on "current" tests.

Enhanced Campaigns (treated as a singular noun) is Google's approach to running ads across multiple devices. In the real world there's no reason to know anything about the way anything worked before the change but in Examland there is. There are old questions still lurking on the test, mostly about targeting, bidding, and mobile ads. Whenever that's an issue, I'll make an exam-centered comment about the old way and quickly move on.

These exams assume the test-taker is a search engine marketer who works at an agency and manages someone else's AdWords spend. If you're in-house at an e-commerce property, then you'll be asked some questions that are based on the kind of experience you do not have (like dealing with clients). If you're a non-profit marketer or work solely on political campaigns, then you'll face questions about things (like ROI) that you'll have to prepare for by reviewing the same materials as the inexperienced new arrival.

How Current is This?

This material will be out of date the moment it's published. Google will never finish building AdWords or rotating new questions into the exam, so I'll never finish writing this guide. You're reading version 1.2 which I want to be the most reliable resource of its kind. It'll be updated often and only the latest edition will be available (as past editions are removed from points of sale). To see what's changed since this version was created, visit the guides' home at SearchCerts.com.

As just covered, the opposite problem also exists in that you might face a test question about a feature Google discontinued years ago. Not all outdated questions have been purged, so you may see some which are correctly answered in ways that have recently become wrong. I wouldn't be doing right by you by not mentioning that such questions are still in circulation when you could possibly face one (or a few). To serve you well, the policy in effect here is: If I've seen a question on an exam in the last 12 months, then it's covered, even if it should not rightfully still be in circulation.

In a seeming contradiction, this guide gets updated frequently because the test is updated frequently and it's outdated because the test is outdated. The guide doesn't care what's going on in the real world, only about what you'll face on the test.

The exam is (in part) meant to test your ability to conform to Google's best practices, so we'll follow them to the letter. Some methods or answers might not apply to the real world and anyone experienced in AdWords will certainly read more than one practice here that she wouldn't use on a live account. Whenever and wherever you spot such a difference, please bear in mind that this is an exam prep guide which presents the "test way" of doing things. After passing your exam, you can go right back to running AdWords however you want.

This guide is for the US version of the exam. There are others and the difference between them is more than just the spelling of "optimize" versus "optimise." Different versions are *nearly* identical, but the two areas where there are most likely to be differences are policy questions (like ads related to gambling) and geographic targeting questions (like whether individual postal codes can be targeted). If you're taking a version other than the US English one, then be sure to review information about those two topics specific to your domain.

What's New About the New Test?

The current version of this guide was revised in early 2014, a few months after the launch of the Google Partners Program that replaced the Google Certified Partner program. This portion is meant to give a heads-up about what's changed since then to anyone who's familiar with the old tests, so if you've *never* taken the exams then you could skip past this section and go right to Chapter 2.

If you're taking a renewal, then you want to be aware of how different the test is now than it was when you last took it. The differences in the content of the new test are completely covered in Part II. The differences in the actual functionality of the testing platform are covered right here.

First, exams are now free of charge for all. It used to cost US$50 for individuals who were not associated with an agency that participated in certain programs. Those programs have since been combined to form the Google Partners Program and no one pays for tests.

There are exactly 90 questions on the Fundamentals Exam and 99 on the Advanced Search Exam, which is more consistent than the old tests which varied between 95 and 105 questions. The test-taker never knew exactly how many she would face until the test began. It's fairer now because both new and old versions have a 120 minute time limit, so different test-takers used to have different amounts of time per question, depending on how many questions they had to answer in two hours.

Questions which have been seen on the new exam are four-option multiple choice items with only one "correct" answer.

The old tests included "select all that apply" and true/false questions but those formats have not yet been spotted on the new exams. That doesn't mean they're not coming, so those formats are still covered here.

Now there's no back button, no way to mark questions for further review, and no review at all. The testing platform will not allow you to skip a question, leave one unanswered, go back to a previous question, or return to a question later for further review. The new *Confirm Answer* button will remain subdued and un-clickable until you pick an answer and only then will it allow you to proceed. Once you answer a question, you'll never see it again. The old exam allowed test-takers to go back and see previously answered questions and use spare time at the end to review all answers before submission. The new one does not.

There is no strikethrough feature either. The old exam allowed test-takers to right-click on an answer choice to "cross it out" which assisted in eliminating incorrect answer choices in order to narrowly consider only the remaining options.

Google used to employ a third-party company named Internet Testing Systems whose testing platform allowed for these features. The new tests are hosted on Google's own App Engine and have no such features. On balance, most changes are mostly beneficial, but there are some steep downsides. The new version is even less friendly to those who don't typically do well on standardized tests.

CHAPTER 2: Individual Certification Types

The *Google Partners Program* is Google's AdWords certification body. A program *member* is anyone who signs-up for a Partner Program account. A *Certified Individual* is any member who passes the Fundamentals Exam and one of the two advanced exams. Neither members nor certified individuals have to work at a Partner company or meet any other requirements.

A *Partner Company* (sometimes just called a *Google Partner*) is the company-level certification and only companies (not people) can be described as Google's "Partners." Individual people can only say they're certified but aren't supposed to use the title "Partner."

Who Certifies & Why

A company employing certified people doesn't have to be a Google Partner, but if it is then at least one person must maintain the individual-level certification.

Maybe the certification will reassure clients of the level of service they'd get from you. Sometimes certification is for client-facing roles (like sales) in which talking-shop with the client's marketing person makes the difference in their choice of which agency to hire.

Other times, account managers who never actually see a client certify so everyone can be assured the individual person assigned to optimize an account is competent. Some prospective clients will be impressed by the certification and many don't care.

Maybe you are not yet working in performance marketing and certification will demonstrate pay-per-click proficiency to potential employers. There are colleges that nudge students to certify so they'll enter the market with a better résumé. The expectation in such a case is not that they could know their way around an AdWords account, but that on-the-job training won't start on day one with explanations as basic as "Google is a search engine. A search engine is..."

The MCC Requirement

An *SEM* (Search Engine Marketing) agency might be hired to run AdWords on behalf of very different clients like a car leasing company, an online clothing retailer, and a regional board of tourism. *My Client Center* (MCC - also known as *Multi-Client Center*) is designed so a marketer can login to one place and work on these three different AdWords accounts while keeping them and their budgets completely separate.

The Partners program *almost* requires that every individual person be linked to an MCC account. It is not absolutely necessary, but Google will make it unnecessarily difficult to take advantage of the program if you don't.

Not everyone who has a reason to certify really needs an MCC account. In-house people in client-side marketing departments have a legitimate reason to individually certify, but no compelling reason to run accounts under an MCC. Everyone with an AdWords account already has a ghost MCC that lies unused and never-logged-into. You should activate yours so it can be linked to your Partner Program account (covered soon) which needs to be created before taking any exams.

Whichever email address you use to access the MCC is the one you want to use when you first sign up as an individual member of the Partners program. Google will automatically recognize it and link the two.

If you use any other email address for Partners, then you'll have to go to your MCC account and "invite yourself" by sending an invitation to become an administrator to the email you used for Partners and then login to that account and accept your own invitation. Unless you have a good reason, this is a headache to avoid by using the same email address in both.

Switching Employers

Maybe your individual certification is attached to the Partner company you work for and you're considering another job offer. If you want to walk your certified self across the street, then your individual qualification is yours, as it represents what you know and have achieved. Your personal certification wouldn't need to be transferred anywhere, but your Partner Program portal login privileges (covered soon) will need updating.

If your new employer is also a Google Partner company, it'll benefit from having you on the payroll counting towards its status. Wanting one more certified person to secure their company-level status may even be the deciding factor in choosing *you* to hire.

Any AdWords certified person can create a new company-level Partner account, as long as she's not currently linked under an existing one. Each person can only be associated with one company account at a time.

Maybe you're a lone wolf consultant who offers independent search engine marketing services or does freelance side work. If you're feeling entrepreneurial then you can create a new Partner company account for yourself – assuming your client list meets the spending threshold of US$10,000 every 90 days. If the total AdWords spending under your control is less than that threshold, then you (as a company) would not qualify for company-level certification, but you (as a person) would maintain individual qualification. You don't have to spend or manage any money at all to be a qualified individual.

So what happens to your old company after you've left? A Google Partner company keeps its status as long as there is one certified person under the roof. If there's only one lone certified individual at a small boutique agency, then that person is an administrator by default.

If the sole administrator leaves the account without first assigning a replacement, then Google warns it could delete the company account and all related data. If your departure leaves a company short, then they'll probably task another person with filling the void. You (the administrator) would add her as an administrator before you leave.

It's also possible if you quit your job and take clients with you that your old employer could be left with accounts that total less than the spending threshold for company-level Partner status. If you did that, then your old company would have to scramble to bring in new money or risk losing their status. You probably wouldn't be spoken of very highly in those halls any more. The performance marketing world is a small one, so be nice.

Certification Envy & Know-It-Alls

Some people actually discourage others from pursuing AdWords certification. Not everyone who's not certified has Certification Envy, but those who do will identify themselves by saying things like "certifications are for kids." You might even hear "Real SEMs don't need certifications because they instead overwhelm prospective clients with case studies, resume info, years of experience, describing prior results at length, a thick dossier, etc., etc., etc..."

One of the most commonly distributed pieces of marketing advice is "Your customers don't want to learn all about you, so you must quickly convey a unique differentiator that benefits them or they will tune out." Those suffering from Certification Envy should take this advice that they surely have given others before.

Has anyone ever had a client who wasn't interested in reading their case studies to discover how amazing they are? Yep. I don't know why someone would actively avoid proving his knowledge in a subject he claims expertise in.

Not every steak with a USDA inspection stamp is good, but I wouldn't buy one that didn't have one. Not every university that's accredited is good, but I wouldn't recommend one that is not. Just as not every PPC manager with an AdWords certification is good, I wouldn't recommend one who doesn't have it. There is nothing noble or sophisticated about *not* being certified.

If you ask around about certification you're even more likely to hear a know-it-all remark: "I passed the test and didn't even try." Such a comment doesn't provide you with meaningful information, but is purely a social positioning statement. He's trying to put you down with his real message: "It's easier for me because I'm smarter than you."

Someone who says "I passed it in my sleep" has identified himself as being more concerned with being better than you and less concerned with giving you real information. I hope those who say "I got certified without even trying" aren't as dismissive of their clients as they are with their peers.

CHAPTER 3: Company Certification Types

For a company to qualify as a Partner, it must have at least one AdWords certified person, manage at least US$10,000 every 90 days under its MCC, and that MCC must be at least 90 days old. Those are the criteria. If you want to morph your company into a search engine marketing firm (or at least expand that part of your mix), then the spending threshold might be a barrier if your company is not already handling that much AdWords volume.

Promoting to Prospects

Of all the benefits of certification, Google has got the idea that the most sought-after carrot they're holding is "The Badge," an online link to an image of a badge that an agency can display on their website. There's no badge for individuals. Most Partners literature is written in badge-centered language which describes it as the actual purpose of certifying.

The badge can be displayed on Partner companies' websites, marketing materials, linked Google+ pages, and even business cards and letterhead. It comes in the form of embeddable HTML which means Google can measure how it gets viewed and remotely alter or remove it. If you're thinking it'd be easy to simply paste a badge image onto your company's site without Google finding out, then you're underestimating their ability to find things on the Internet.

The *Google Partner Profile page* is something you'll want to opt-in to and link to from your web properties, social media pages, and just about everything else except for email signatures (which they frown on).

The *Google Partner Portal* is the central place to manage qualifying factors like individual employees' certification statuses and access Google-approved marketing materials which will ensure you don't run afoul of any of their "don't say you and us are too cozy" policies. Because the Google Partner Program, Google Partner Profile, and Google Partner Portal all share the same initials, we'll avoid abbreviating any of them to avoid confusion.

Few things seem to madden Googlers more than marketers who tell clients they have a special relationship with Google and some special access that others don't. Most of the policies about marketing your or your company's certification are meant to stop you from exaggerating how close you are to Google. Refer to their own materials for updated policy details, but the theme is that you will not "display the logo in any manner that implies a relationship or affiliation with Google or sponsorship or endorsement by Google."

The Partner Program account is linked to an agency's MCC which Google uses to judge that agency's spending and ensure it at least passes their threshold of US$10,000 to qualify. If your company runs more than one MCC, you can create a parent MCC to link them under so your company gets credit for every dollar it passes to AdWords. One agency can't have two profiles and two agencies can't share one profile. First, get your MCC straight. Then, create a Partners account to link to it.

The individual people logging in to the portal are designated as either *administrators* or *members*. Every person under a company's profile contributes to that company's status. Administrators can invite new employees in to the portal and will get messages whenever one takes an exam or if someone's individual certification will expire soon.

Google Partner Search

The "Find a Google Partner" page of the Partner portal is an advertiser-facing database of certified companies. Google claims they actively drive traffic to the page from links within the AdWords dashboard, help center pages, and house ads. Partners certification puts a company into the database, making it findable by prospective clients. Your company's listing there might just be your highest-authority and hardest-won link.

A profile page contains agency-entered info like locations, logo, and a descriptive paragraph. When registering, you'll have to choose from lists of industries your company serves, which services you offer, which languages you support, which countries you service, and the minimum budget you're willing to handle (it can be $0). If you choose not to answer these then your company would not show up in searches because you're not giving any parameters for user searches to be matched to. Google also lists how many people in the organization have which individual certifications.

The sequence of Partners search results is manipulated. Company-level Partner accounts have a *Partner Rating* score based on "best practices campaign strength" which will partially determine position in results. The way to manipulate your Partner Rating is to conform to all of Google's best practices and accept all of their recommendations. You'll get automated suggestions for raising your Partner Rating which are meant to encourage you to encourage your clients to accept the recommendations.

They'll even present you with canned presentation materials and literature to persuade both you and your clients to do everything Google's way. The Partner portal also contains a library of marketing materials designed to help you sell AdWords in accordance with Google policy.

If Google sends you leads from the Find a Partner page and you take a long time (according to them) to respond to the prospect, then your company will appear lower in future results. Google is also tracking how many of the leads it sends you later become clients by tracking who they send you and who later shows-up as a client under your MCC.

If you're not being honest about your minimum spending threshold, this is how they'll find that out also. Some may be tempted to exaggerate their minimum spending threshold to falsely inflate prestige. If your profile says your company only accepts clients who are spending at least $50,000 per month while your MCC is full of those spending $500 per month, then Google knows what you're doing.

Promotional Offers

A linked MCC is necessary for a Partner company to have access to promotional offers to pass on to new clients. The idea is that you are now armed with incentives to bring new advertisers to AdWords. This is not to be confused with *Google Offers* which is (or was) a consumer-oriented Groupon clone.

Visiting the *Offers* dashboard (within the Partners Portal) will trigger AdWords to scan the accounts under your company's MCC to see if there are any that fit the description of the kinds of advertisers they're currently making promotional offers to. These offers vary by country and you can only give them to prospects or clients located in the same country as your agency. You can't apply offers to your own agency's AdWords usage to promote itself, so no free house ads. Anything other than giving the credit to an advertiser client to encourage them to advertise on AdWords is against their rules.

Badge Revocability

One reason for the certifications' existence is that performance marketing is infamous as an industry where everyone claims they're experts though no one has any credentials. There are too many know-it-alls. How is an advertiser to know who's competent enough to hire? Self-appointed search experts are out there evangelizing AdWords which benefits Google. But Google doesn't want them butchering clients' PPC efforts, leading to the feeling among advertisers that AdWords just doesn't work.

The biggest threat to the value of the Partner Program is every time an advertiser gets burned by the sloppy work of someone who has the qualification. Google's approach to revoking badges is based on signals it finds inside the AdWords and MCC accounts of certified individuals and Partner companies. They harvest this data to identify sloppy work, which is grounds for revoking the badge. They specifically mention a lack of negative keywords and Sitelinks as red flags they look for. If the accounts we manage don't have them, then Google wonders if it's because we're no good at this.

If your company is in danger of such a defrocking, expect a sternly-worded email. You can also opt-in to *Performance Suggestions* emails (in the Partners portal) which are automatically-generated periodic emails that list things Google wants you to do differently. These can act as an early warning system to tip you off that something in your MCC has raised their attention.

This approach to badge revocability will go a long way to reassure the world that hiring a certified individual or Partner company ensures they're not hiring a lousy one.

CHAPTER 4: The Exams

If you've never seen the exams, you must want to know: What's on them? If you're up for a renewal, then your concern must be: How new is "new?" This chapter covers the nuts-and-bolts of the new exams, the format, question types, and we'll see a few sample questions.

About the Exams

In the AdWords certification universe, there are two certifications based on three tests. To become certified, you'll take the Fundamentals Exam and then either the Advanced Search Exam or the Advanced Display Exam. Each option results in an AdWords Search or Display Certification, or you can obtain both by passing all three tests.

There's also the completely separate Google Analytics Individual Qualification (GAIQ) Exam and the AdSense Certification Exam and both of those are completely different animals that have nothing to do with AdWords certification or each other.

Google says its Fundamentals Exam covers "basic aspects of AdWords and online advertising, including account management and the value of search advertising." A passing score is good for two years before it must be renewed. The Search Exam covers "managing AdWords campaigns" while the Display Exam covers "advertising on YouTube and the Google Content Network." Each of the advanced exams expire in one year so each one of those must be renewed annually. To put a point on that: Although the Fundamentals Exam is good for two years, the Advanced Exams are each good for just one.

You'll see your score the moment you finish the test. The passing score varies by exam and the Fundamentals has the highest threshold, requiring a score of 85% to pass. The Search Exam requires 80% to pass while the Display Exam requires only 70%.

Focus Effort on What Counts

Now is the time to set a goal: Do you just want to pass or do you want to pass with a great score? There are two different strategies and deciding if your goal is to pass or to pass with a great score makes the difference in whether you can ignore one topic or need to absorb encyclopedic knowledge.

The Ignore One Topic Strategy

If all you want is to pass and you don't care about your score, then you can focus on the topics that are relevant to you in the real world more heavily than those you'll probably never see outside of the exam. You have less ability to do this in the Fundamentals Exam than other exams because the pass rate of 85% is so high. You can't ignore too much like you could if you only had to answer 70% of the questions correctly for the Advanced Display Exam.

What if chopping off 5% of the material could shorten your prep time and effort by 15%? Please be aware that you can't cut off 50% of this material and expect to pass, so don't ignore all display advertising because you plan to certify in search. I'd suspect that as the number one reason people fail the Fundamentals Exam.

For the Ignore One Topic Strategy to work, the one topic you choose to ignore must be one that's too narrow and small to supply very many questions to the exam. Skip whichever one sub-section you feel would take the most time to master and be the least useful to you after test day. Maybe you work only on lead generation accounts so you don't care about Product Listing Ads. Maybe you're a few rungs below the MCC administrator at an agency so you doubt that MCC management will matter to you. This strategy is only useful if it's important to you to spend as little time as possible on exam prep and a barely-passing score is acceptable.

The Encyclopedic Knowledge Strategy

The biggest AdWords advertisers are buying a variety of products from Google, much more than just CPC (cost-per-click) text ads on google.com. If you want to be entrusted to handle such a large and complex account, then prove your capability by getting a super score. If you work for a Partner agency, the account administrator (and probably your boss) will see your scores and you can't afford to just barely pass. Likewise, if you're not yet working at a performance marketing agency but want to, then showboat some serious search engine chops by scoring higher than others who already work in the field.

The Encyclopedic Knowledge Strategy is to learn the entire breadth of AdWords. Spend lots of time and effort on the areas you see least. If you want a perfect or near-perfect score, then don't skip anything.

And, don't stop here. YouTube is full of tutorials and dashboard walk-throughs so you can see how things like Manager Defined Spend work, even if you personally don't have administrator access to a live account to try it out yourself. One caveat: Almost all tutorials are intended for use in the real world. Sometimes a practice which you should absolutely follow when there is real money on the line is different than what Google wants you to do, and the exam is a test of how well you know what Google wants you to do. Online tutorials are reliable for step-by-step instructions of things like how to properly set geographic targeting options, but not for the "why" questions involving how you "should" handle things like bid strategy.

Clever Kevin Traps

Earlier we met Clever Kevin and the time has come for a formal introduction. You've met people like him before. When he first began learning AdWords he kept inventing ways to out-Google Google and he insists that he's the first person to ever think of the things he thinks of. He believes the Internet full of holes that somehow only he can exploit. He also has this idea that AdWords offers him a platform to trick gullible Internet users without Google noticing.

Clever Kevin's intentions aren't always malicious, as sometimes he just mismanages a client's budget because he thinks optimization is simpler than it is. One way for Google to wake him up is to fail him on a test, so we'll have to recognize the exam's Clever Kevin traps.

Just as Google wants to indoctrinate the world's marketers to follow Google's best practices, they also want to put an end to worst practices and one of those tools is the AdWords certification program. Worst practices are all those things that Google wishes Clever Kevin didn't do so if there's an answer choice that involves doing them, then eliminate it immediately. Tactics to screw Internet users, competitors, or Google, and anything that smells spammy are all things that will always be wrong on all AdWords exams. Always! Wherever the name *Clever Kevin* appears after this, it's *italicized* to draw attention to a trap or misconception of some sort.

Question Styles

AdWords exam items are multiple-choice questions with four options to select a single answer from. They're selected by clicking a round radio button, the kind that will be unselected if you subsequently clicked another option. They are no different than the format you've probably seen throughout your early life in school:

1. An English-speaking user in Hong Kong who has set his Google interface language to Simplified Chinese performs a search using Korean characters on www.google.cn. In which language will AdWords serve ads?
   o Korean
   o Simplified Chinese
   o English
   o Cantonese

Korean is one of only five languages identified based solely on its unique alphabet, which will override any conflicting indicators about language, which leads us to the first choice. Notice that choices are not labeled A, B, C, and D as they traditionally are. That's how they'll appear on the exam.

Other questions could ask you to "select all that apply," instructing you to choose more than one check box. Recent tests have not had any like this, but that doesn't mean they won't appear as the new Partners Program matures. Don't be surprised to see one like this:

1. Ellen has one top-level MCC with two sub-levels for her employees Joe and John. Each of the two individual sub-level MCCs has its own MDO. Ellen wants to move the Acme account from Joe to John. Which of the following are concerns? Select all that apply.
   ☐ There must first be a sub-level MCC that is accessible to John but not Joe to which Ellen can move the managed account
   ☐ Conversion Tracking must also be migrated to John's sub-level MCC
   ☐ All data will be lost if Ellen does not first back it up in AdWords Editor
   ☐ The Acme account will lose funding unless the MDO is also moved

The first and last options are both concerns, so they must both be selected for this item to be correct. The material you actually need to know for the exam is covered in Part II, so don't worry if these sample questions in Part I don't make sense yet.

There could also be true/false questions which have been more prevalent on the Advanced Display Exam than others. Bear in mind the options aren't always ordered in the expected way, with the first option being True and the second option being False. They're sometimes reversed like the example below. Give at least one moment of attention to this before answering a true/false item:

1. The default CPC bidding option is Automatic CPC bidding.
   o FALSE
   o TRUE

CPC bidding is manual by default, so this statement is false.

The exact same question may appear more than once in the same exact test. This has happened in about a third of the exams taken to research this guide. Answer choices are presented in random order so the same options appear in a different sequence on subsequent servings of the same question. The first sample item we just saw might be question number 14 during an exam session:

14. An English-speaking user in Hong Kong who has set his Google interface language to Simplified Chinese performs a search using Korean characters on www.google.cn. In which language will AdWords serve ads?
   o Korean
   o Simplified Chinese
   o English
   o Cantonese

And then later during that exact same exam session, it could appear again as question number 81 with answer choices in a different order:

81. An English-speaking user in Hong Kong who has set his Google interface language to Simplified Chinese performs a search using Korean characters on www.google.cn. In which language will AdWords serve ads?
   o English
   o Korean
   o Cantonese
   o Simplified Chinese

If you're confident in your answer to a repeated question, then this phenomenon benefits your score because your correct answer is correct twice. But if you feel less confident about your answer to a repeated question, then your only course of action when seeing it the second time is to reexamine it as a fresh question. There is no way to return to an old question to change an already submitted answer.

The randomized answer sequence also means that "none of the above" is reworded as "none of these options is correct" so that the null option will still be valid when served in any of the four slots. Imagine if "none of the above" were (by chance) served as the first option like this:

1. Which of the following goals is appropriate for an uncapped budget?
   o None of the above
   o To increase offline sales at a brick-and-mortar physical clothing store
   o To increase online sales at an office supply e-commerce website
   o To increase web traffic for a public health campaign with a fixed budget

The phrase "none of these options is correct" fixes the problem created when answers are randomly sequenced:

1. Which of the following goals is appropriate for an uncapped budget?
   o None of these options is correct
   o To increase offline sales at a brick-and-mortar physical clothing store
   o To increase online sales at an office supply e-commerce website
   o To increase web traffic for a public health campaign with a fixed budget

If none of the options were correct, then the wording of the first answer choice would make sense in any of the four positions. But, the third choice in this sample question is an appropriate goal for an uncapped budget and correctly answers this question.

Math is Not All That Hard

Have a calculator by your side, even though only one or two questions per exam call for a calculation of any kind. Topics like Bidding and Quality Score lend themselves to questions that require some basic arithmetic. Let's look at one which requires you to combine adjustments.

1. If you set a default Max CPC bid of $1.00 for your ads, and set a +25% Bid Adjustment for weekends and a +100% Bid Adjustment for mobile ads, then what is your Max bid after adjustments when both conditions apply?
   - o $2.25
   - o $2.50
   - o $3.25
   - o $1.00

That's the most math-heavy question imaginable on the test. First, the $1.00 default CPC is adjusted up by +25% to $1.25. Then, that $1.25 is adjusted up +100% to $2.50, which is the second answer choice.

The math itself is more straight-forward than the definitions of terms needed to identify what kind of result you're being asked to produce. In Examland you'll encounter acronyms that aren't often used in the real world. Some test takers might need to familiarize themselves with less-used ones, such as CPI (Cost-per-Interaction or Cost-per-Install).

Most numbers-filled questions aren't asking you to calculate anything, but they're really looking to see if you know a numbers-related definition:

1. You set the CPM of a keyword on the Display Network to $10. How much will you pay for 1,000 impressions?
   - o $100
   - o $1,000
   - o $10
   - o $1

There's nothing to do here, because it's only necessary to know that CPM means cost-per-thousand-impressions. 1,000 impressions at a rate of $10 per 1,000 impressions cost $10.

There will almost certainly be at least one question that simply asks you to identify the appropriate equation among similar but incorrect alternatives:

1. Which formula best describes ROI?
    o (Revenue + Cost) * Cost
    o (Revenue - Cost) * Cost
    o (Revenue + Cost) / Cost
    o (Revenue - Cost) / Cost

Google's cookie-cutter ROI formula is to subtract advertising costs from revenue and then divide the result by that same cost number which is shown in the fourth option. This is the exact situation that would call for using the strikethrough tactic that we'll see soon. The take-away is that most "math" questions are really vocabulary questions.

You Don't Need to Crack Google

Stop reading speculation about the dark inner-workings of AdWords! At least for a while. For the purposes of certification exams, it doesn't really matter how the AdWords black box works. We just have to know how Google publically says it works.

The algorithms underlying auctions are often speculated on, especially the more abstract ones like eCPM calculations. They're sure to be both top secret and mind-blowingly complex. But, top-secret factors have zero chance of showing up on an AdWords exam.

If Google is deliberately evasive about something, then we can be sure there will be no test questions about it. Don't sabotage yourself with concern about how Google "really" works. The correct answers to exam questions will always be things that Google wants everyone to know.

CHAPTER 5: Tactics & Counter-Tactics

This chapter focuses on tactics related to specific kinds of questions you'll face and counter-tactics when you're confronted with poorly written questions.

Google's Best Answer

Any person familiar with search engine marketing has previously encountered a real world problem that could be solved in several different ways, and had to choose the best solution for that particular instance. In the same way, you'll encounter exam problems that have more than one fundamentally correct answer, but only one that's "best."

In Examland you're not always trying to pick the real best answer, but Google's best answer. This does not mean that all best answers financially favor Google such as "raise CPCs" or "uncap that budget already." It means if an answer is factually correct but you know Google wishes everyone did something in a different way, then pause and consider all choices before answering.

These exams test how closely your view of AdWords aligns with Google's view of AdWords. Some questions are correctly answered in ways that you don't agree with. Some people believe in dayparting their campaigns and others don't. Google offers a tool for it and the answer they will count as correct is the one that involves using their tool.

No matter how you feel about the issue, Google believes both their search and display networks are great places for branding efforts. Keep that in mind if you were to be asked:

1. Which campaign type is appropriate for brand advertising?
   o Search Network Only
   o Search and Display Networks
   o Display Network Only
   o None of these options is correct

Of course the second answer is the one they're looking for.

Sometimes Google's best answer is factually incorrect. The subjectivity of a "best answer" can be frustrating or it can be managed, so if there is none then choose the least-worst answer. In this next example (below), all answers are outright wrong except for the second one, which is only half wrong, making it the least-worst answer:

1. Which of these ad formats can be shown on the Search Network Only?
   o Image ads
   o Text ads
   o Video ads
   o Rich media ads

They're all wrong. Text ads can also be shown on both the Search and Display Networks, so it's the answer they'd be looking for here.

Clock Watching Tactic

Clever Kevin smiles whenever he considers the prospect of an Internet-mediated test. He thinks he just might be the first person to ever think of sitting down with two screens and testing on one while looking up all the answers on the other. Why hasn't anyone ever thought of this before?

Looking up answers takes longer than knowing answers, and the time limit will keep this from working very well. 90 or more questions can be answered in two hours by someone who knows the answers. They can't be answered in that time by someone who's cranking his neck off to one side looking at endless help menus and hoping the next answer is just behind the next click.

Keep this very guide close at hand when testing, but don't rely on the ability to search for answers. There should be no expectation that just anyone can sit down in front of two computers and look-up each answer for a perfect score. Just anyone would run out of time.

The exams' creators went out of their way to design the current testing platform to responsively conform to any screen size so the tests are doable on a phone screen. That should prove that they're not worried about freeing-up a computer monitor for you to use two screens. They must be confident that there's not enough time for an unfamiliar person to ace the test that way.

Having said that, the time limit is not so severe that there's need to speed-read. You'll have enough time to fully evaluate every question and answer choice, and you should. The first answer choice may be correct, but a subsequent one may be *more correct* (or "best"). Don't pick the first plausible one and move on without even reading the remaining choices due to time limit fears.

If you've previously taken the Google Analytics Qualified Individual Exam, then you might expect AdWords tests to have the same pause feature, but they do not. Once the test starts, the clock keeps ticking.

Strikethrough Tactic

The same process of elimination technique that you'll remember from school is useful here. The current test has no strikethrough feature to aid you in eliminating choices like the old testing platform did. Use old-fashioned scratch paper and the old-fashioned process of elimination. Even if answer choices are not labeled A, B, C, and D, you can use those labels anyway to keep track on real paper of which ones you can safely eliminate. This is especially useful when evaluating answer choices with multiple clauses. Let's narrow one down:

1. If you changed the match type of a keyword from broad match to exact match, you should expect:
   o A lower CTR and a higher volume
   o A higher CTR and a lower volume
   o A lower CTR and a lower volume
   o A higher CTR and a higher volume

It's entirely possible a person who is well aware of the impact of widening or narrowing match types would not pick the right answers to this question because of the way answers are presented. Start eliminating based only on the first portion of the answer. Imagine this is all you saw:

1. If you changed the match type of a keyword from broad match to exact match, you should expect:
   o ~~A lower CTR~~…
   o A higher CTR…
   o ~~A lower CTR~~…
   o A higher CTR…

We can eliminate the first and third choices based just on the first portion of the answers because we know that narrower match types generally produce a higher CTR. Continue eliminating based only on the second portion of the answer, as if all you saw was:

1. If you changed the match type of a keyword from broad match to exact match, you should expect:
   o …~~a higher volume~~
   o …a lower volume
   o …a lower volume
   o …~~a higher volume~~

We can now eliminate the first and last choices because we expect a narrower match type to produce lower volume. If the remaining possibilities are true, then you have your answer. Carefully relook at what's left, and pick:

1. If you changed the match type of a keyword from broad match to exact match, you should expect:
   o ~~A lower CTR~~ and ~~a higher volume~~
   o A higher CTR and a lower volume
   o ~~A lower CTR~~ and a lower volume
   o A higher CTR and ~~a higher volume~~

Narrowing the match type will result in a higher CTR because ads are only shown to the most relevant queries. The lower number of impressions will also result in lower volume. Both of these effects are found in our one remaining answer, the second option.

Managing Helpful Test Traits

There are times when your right answer would be counted wrong because there's something wrong with the exam. There are other times when there's something wrong with the exam that can point you towards the correct answer. In this section, we'll review how to take advantage of helpful question design traits and next we'll see how to prevent being hurt by harmful ones.

Many question/answer combinations are designed to be two clauses of the same sentence, when the question begins a statement and the correct answer finishes it. You can often eliminate choices that (as the end of a sentence) don't grammatically agree with the question (as the beginning of a sentence). An example:

1. Specific Reach is a targeting method in which:
   o Individual IP addresses are targeted.
   o Scheduled delivery of specific dayparts.
   o A specific geographic area is targeted.
   o Both keywords and placements are used.

The second option could not be the second half of the sentence begun in the question portion. Picking it would result in the nonsense sentence: "Specific Reach is a targeting method in which scheduled delivery of specific dayparts." Joining these two clauses does not result in a coherent sentence, so this choice can *probably* be eliminated before considering the remainders. Of those, *Specific Reach* is Googlese for contextual targeting in which both keywords and placements are used. If you weren't certain about this one and dayparting seemed like a plausible answer, then attention to grammatical inconsistencies can help narrow down the options.

Most poorly-constructed answer choices are probably wrong. When constructing a test, it's natural for the test-maker to be less attentive to the wrong answer choices than the correct one. If one of them is gibberish (like the second choice below), then it's under suspicion for being a poor copy/paste job and a good candidate for elimination as an answer choice:

1. AdWords Discounter:
   o Calculates the Actual CPC or CPM to be paid
   o Offer offers new advertiser
   o Finds the lowest priced clicks
   o Discounts clicks when campaign budgets are uncapped

You could at least eliminate the second option without knowing anything about the subject. The first one is correct, but if someone had no idea, then guessing from three would give better odds than guessing from four. However, some poorly-worded answers are correct. If an answer doesn't pair well with a question (like the third one below), then you should suspect that it *could* be wrong but don't thoughtlessly eliminate it *solely* for that reason.

1. You set Ad Rotation to Rotate Evenly. You should then expect Ad Rotation to:
   o Optimize for conversions after 60 days
   o Rotate ads indefinitely
   o Begins to optimize for clicks after 90 days
   o Optimize for conversions after 90 days

Although mistakes in answer choices can assist you in narrowing down the field, this can qualify as a harmful test trait when the test-makers' error can mislead you to eliminate a correct answer. That could happen with the third choice above, which is correct though grammatically flawed.

Managing Harmful Test Traits

Beware of negatively-phrased questions. Sometimes you're looking for the only one that's *not* right:

1. Exact Match will not:
   o be the default option
   o match plural forms
   o match variants
   o be designated by the use of brackets

Exact match is designated by the use of [brackets] and will match plural forms and variants of keywords. The only one that is not true is the first option because exact match is not the default match type. In this one, we deliberately identify and select the choice that's *incorrect* for a negatively phrased question.

Beware of changes in voice, tone, or tense which can cloud the question. These are not the most skillfully crafted questions and inconsistencies like this are common:

1. An advertiser wants to temporarily suspend advertising one of her products. She should consider that when an ad group is paused:
   o All previous performance data is deleted
   o The ads it contains will not be reviewed until it is un-paused
   o All ads within the same ad group are paused
   o All ads within the same campaign are paused

The passive wording of "when an ad group is paused" makes it less than clear that our advertiser (and not Google) is the one who's doing the pausing. Regardless of who pauses an ad group, all ads within it are paused so the third statement is the only true one.

Beware of questions containing words that infer important information, but don't say it directly. The word "placements" should immediately tip you off that this question is about the Display Network:

1. Quality Score of a placement is based on:
   o The past performance on mobile devices
   o Clickthrough-rate (CTR)
   o Landing page experience
   o The past performance in a designated geographic area

The Question could have read "Quality Score *on the Display Network* is based on…" and still lead to the same answer. That was also an example of an item composed of two clauses which create a true sentence when the correct "answer" (landing page experience) is selected.

Beware of questions which use "quotation marks" for no good reason, which can cause confusion. Quotation marks are used in Google's exam questions (and in this guide) in the same way they're used in all the rest of the English language. But they're also used within the AdWords dashboard to designate *phrase match* keywords. Be mindful that such marks around a keyword do not always indicate phrase match is in play, like this one:

1. Which of these queries would your keyword "water skis" be eligible for if you set it to exact match?
   o Water and boating skis
   o Lake water skis
   o Water skiing
   o Water skis on sale

The deliberate mention of *exact match* should override any thought that the quotation marks are designating a phrase match keyword. The third choice includes the term skiing which is a variant of skis without any other terms, so it's the only option that exact match would serve an ad on.

Beware of obsolete questions. The *Traffic Estimator* and *Keyword Tool* don't exist anymore, but that doesn't mean all questions about them have been purged from the exam:

1. You are conducting keyword research. The Traffic Estimator is a free tool used to estimate:
    o The incoming traffic of the keywords in an ad group
    o The volume and costs of keywords
    o Your ad position for selected keywords
    o The traffic your competitors receive on a keyword

The Traffic Estimator previously estimated keyword volume and costs before it was replaced by the *Keyword Planner*. The second choice correctly answers the question even though it no longer applies in the real world.

CHAPTER 6: Test Day

This chapter covers test registration and what to expect from the testing platform. All the following chapters of Part II will cover the actual content of what you need to know for the test.

First Time Registration

You need to register on the Google Partners Program portal before you can take any of the exams. You can create and edit your Partner Program profile whether certified or not, with or without having an AdWords or MCC account. It doesn't cost anything and you won't have to run any ads on a live account.

The process is more seamless if you sign-up using a Gmail address but you don't have to. Once you enter a primary email address, you can add others, but Google will not allow you to remove any later.

After the Terms of Service you'll be asked about your job function, and then your "interest" in different channels, countries, and industries. You can leave these blank if you like. Inside the portal, under certifications you'll see three exams, the Fundamentals, Advanced Search and Advanced Display. To attempt one, click it and proceed to that test's details page.

The Test Begins

All the usual test-taking advice applies so please don't forget that scratch paper and calculator, with fresh batteries if it takes them. If you're taking the exam on a device that's not physically plugged in to a wall, then be sure it's charged. The testing site is responsively designed so you can take it on your tablet or phone, if your thumbs are up to it.

Take the test from home if you can get two distraction-free hours. If you have to slip away from the keyboard for a break, you can just walk off without the fear of getting cornered in a workplace hallway conversation and explaining that there's a test timer counting down in your cubicle that you really need to get back to.

Once you're logged-in to your Google Partners Program portal, follow the path from Certifications --> AdWords --> (your choice of test) --> Take Exam. That last *Take Exam* link will open the testing site hosted on Google's App Engine. You'll see a short set of instructions before actually beginning the test. They'll read:

> *You are about to take the XXX XXX exam.*
>
> *## Questions*
>
> *120 Minutes*
>
> *Once you confirm your answer to any question, you will not be able to change your answer or review the question. If you choose to end the exam early or close your browser window, your progress will not be saved and your exam will not be scored.*

The "##" is a placeholder for the exact number of questions, 90 for the Fundamentals Exam or 99 for the Advanced Search Exam. Below those instructions, you'll see a *Start Exam Now* button. Don't dare press it unless you're ready for the timer's unpauseable countdown. Once you click *Start Exam Now*, you'll find yourself looking at the first question, and your first possible glimpse of the timer will read "Remaining Time: 01:59:59" as it will have already begun.

If the Test doesn't Begin

If the test doesn't begin, then first on the list of things to check is a pop-up blocker or utility, which you can disable for the moment. You could also add the testing site to the whitelist of URLs approved by you to deliver pop-ups. If you use dual monitors then you might be able to allow it to open by reconfiguring to just one active monitor.

If the test begins but the *Confirm Answer* button doesn't appear or the whole thing freezes, then you could try whitelisting the site within your anti-virus or firewall settings. If the pages aren't updating (if clicking *Confirm Answer* from question #1 does not lead to question #2), then caching might not be happening because of some earlier time when you opted-out of it. If so, ensure your browser is set to automatically check the server for the latest page. If none of these suggestions work, then it's time to use the *Help* page's "contact us" feature within the Partner Program portal.

The Test Ends

Once you press *Confirm Answer* on the final question, the test is done and you'll immediately see your score report page which shows the number and percentage of questions correct, and an explicit pass/fail statement, presented like this:

You got ## / ## questions correct. (##%)

Congratulations, you passed the XXX XXX exam.

After a victory dance, the only option is the *Close Exam* button which will return you to the Partner Program portal where you began. That's it. There will be no diagnostic feedback and you will not be shown areas where you could improve.

Once back in the Partner Program portal, you may see "not yet attempted" still under the relevant exam box. If so, don't worry as a delay in posting is common and it's unlikely that there's actually a problem. If your result is not reflected after a few days and you still see "not yet attempted," then it's time to look into it. This is another time to make use of the *Help* page's "contact us" feature.

You are the critic I value most, so share your success story with me. Once you've taken the exam, I want to know what this guide has done for you, where it failed you, and how your actual exam aligned with the expectations set here. Your feedback will improve future editions and I'll happily cite your name and business, and link out to you for any useful tip. Tell me how to make this guide better at keith@keithpenn.com.

Note on the Different Guides in this Series

There are some subjects which appear on both the Fundamentals and Advanced Search Exams. Whenever this happens, the subject is covered by the Fundamentals Exam Prep Guide and material is *not* repeated in the Advanced Search Exam Prep Guide.

The chapters of the Fundamentals Exam Prep Guide which are also needed to be prepared for the Advanced Search Exam are:

CHAPTER 10: Account Structure
CHAPTER 15: Growing a Campaign
CHAPTER 16: How Google Grades Ads
CHAPTER 19: CPA Bid Management
CHAPTER 21: Ad Scheduling
CHAPTER 23: Ad Creation & Formats

There is no Advanced Display Exam Prep Guide at this time. But, the chapters of the Fundamentals Exam Prep Guide which are also needed to be prepared for the Advanced Display Exam are:

CHAPTER 13: Display Targeting
CHAPTER 16: How Google Grades Ads
CHAPTER 19: CPA Bid Management
CHAPTER 20: CPM Bid Management
CHAPTER 23: Ad Creation & Formats

All guides in the SearchCerts.com Exam Prep Series share the exact same Part I that you've just read. Part II exclusively covers the test material this guide is for.

PART II: WHAT'S ON THE SEARCH EXAM

Part I set expectations for test structure, tactics, and clarified what the Google Partner Program, exams, and certifications are all about. Part II is intended solely to prepare you the Google Advanced Search Exam. It assumes you already know everything on the Fundamentals Exam and have already passed it. Nothing here is intended to prepare you for the Display Exam.

The Advanced Search Exam focuses exclusively on search advertising at a level most working professionals would call "intermediate." This is not a guide about advanced AdWords techniques, but about the test which is the second step to become AdWords certified in search.

There won't be any separate practice exam section or question bank because there's already someone out there doing this better than I ever could. iPassExam has more time and resources to dedicate to sample questions and gives them to you in a realistic testing environment. It's a paid service so get the current discount codes at my author site: KeithPenn.com/discounts.

CHAPTER 7: Experiments

There's always something that would perform better than an existing campaign element and an experiment is the way to find out what that is. An advertiser can run several versions of an ad to see which one performs best, and then repeat by creating new ads based on the winner to see which of those variations perform best. Advertisers are also constantly rotating new keywords into campaigns for experimentation and pausing those that perform poorly. This is a constant and never-ending process.

Ideas for experiments can come from you or Google. *AdWords Campaign Experiments* (ACE) is for the ones you think of, while the *Opportunities Tab* presents ideas Google wants you to try. Because it's less involved, the Opportunities Tab is on the Fundamentals Exam and is covered in that guide, while the more-involved ACE feature is on the Search Exam and covered here.

AdWords Campaign Experiments allows an advertiser to measure the difference between an existing (control group) element and a proposed (experimental group) one. The easiest experiment to conceptualize is an ad copy variation, but you can also test whole ad groups, keywords, negative keywords, display URLs, match types, bid levels, and even keyword insertion schemes.

The experiments feature is not a way for *Clever Kevin* to sneak policy-violating ad copy into the AdWords format. Whatever ad he writes as an experimental version is still subject to the same ad status rules as always.

Anything that applies to a whole campaign cannot be tested because AdWords doesn't offer a way to randomly serve variations that apply that widely. All forms of targeting are set at the campaign level, so geographic, language, or network targeting options can't be the subjects of experiments. Neither can a campaign's total budget, ad scheduling, campaign-level ad extensions, or anything else that's set for a whole campaign.

Necessity of Experiments

Experiments find differences in performance by running real ads that cost real money. Nothing is done in simulation. Whether an advertiser creates and experiment in which 500 higher-bid clicks happen or simply raises the bid for the next 500 clicks, she'd pay that higher bid amount in real dollars. So why experiment if the costs and feedback are the same as just changing something in a live account? She'd want to use experiments in situations where it wouldn't be clear if changes to traffic are due to changes in the account or changes in the world.

Let's say we're advertising stock brokerage services at a time when people are increasingly optimistic and selling the gold they've been hanging on to in order to buy stocks. If we just raise bids and see more traffic, then we can't really tell how much of that is due to our raised bid and how much should be attributed to the rising overall demand for what we do. But if we ran an experiment, then we can see how our higher bid is impacting things because we can compare it to the control group. We'd also see exactly how higher demand is driving higher traffic that we'd see even if we made no changes to anything. Such information can't be had without AdWords Campaign Experiments.

Minimizing the Risks of Experiments

Some experiments can be risky. Each time an ad-triggering auction takes place, AdWords will serve either the control or experimental version. If you're testing a broad match keyword that was previously set to exact, then you could pay for lots of clicks that don't convert. The experiments feature itself doesn't cost anything to use, but if an advertiser tests higher CPCs, then she'll pay for the higher CPCs and if she tests something that generates more traffic, then she'll pay for more traffic.

For this reason, you should decide which percentage of auctions should run in the experimental group. Let's say an ad runs on the hypothetical $1.00 CPC and we're going to experiment with a $3.00 CPC with each version running 50% of the time. Of the first thousand clicks, 500 would cost $1.00 each

($500) and the other 500 would cost $3.00 each ($1,500). We'd owe $2,000 total.

It didn't have to be that way. If we would have allocated 75% of our auctions to the control group and only 25% to the experimental group, then those first 1,000 clicks would have generated 750 clicks at $1.00 each ($750) and 250 clicks at $3.00 each ($750). That same experimental period would have cost us $1,500 total. Of course actual ad serving depends on so many factors that we can't predict an exact number of each (like exactly 750 for one or exactly 250 for the other). Those numbers are only here to illustrate.

Setting each group to 50% does not necessarily mean that each ad will be shown 50% of the time. An experimental group with a bid three times higher would probably be seen more often, as that's the whole point of bidding higher. But, when control and experimental groups are set to each show 50/50, factors other than costs can alter that ratio as well. If experimental ad copy receives more clicks than the previous control group's ad copy, then its higher Quality Score will also lead to it being shown more often. Even if both are put into the auction just as often, one could be served on the second *SERP* (Search Engine Results Page) which is seen by fewer users because many don't bother loading it. When this happens, it won't count as having an impression even though AdWords put it up to be served.

If you test variations which perform worse than the pre-existing control group versions, then an experiment can hurt Quality Scores too. Google tries to make us feel better about this possibility by stressing that over the long term, experiments can identify high performers which should raise Quality Scores overall.

Time & Significance

Focusing on *KPIs* (Key Performance Indicators) is central to performing an experiment. To "perform better" means different things to different advertisers, so it's necessary to choose specific metric to measure an experiment by. Is the experimental group better than the control group if it produces more conversions? More clicks? Impressions? Just like any other comparisons, it's necessary to pay attention to what counts and not be distracted by metrics that aren't applicable.

Let's say our primary KPI is *Conversion Rate* and the control and experimental versions each get only 10 clicks during the duration of a test. If one of the control's clicks converted (1 is 10% of 10) and two of the experimental clicks converted (2 is 20% of 10), then does that mean the change is twice as good because it converts at twice the rate (20% vs. 10%)?

While it's true the experimental group here has twice as many conversions, the volume is so low it could be sheer chance behind the numbers. There's not enough *Statistical Significance* and we can't say with any certainty that one group is twice as good as the other. That would change if we had more volume.

If the control group produced 10,000 conversions from 100,000 clicks (10%) and the experimental group produced 20,000 conversions from 100,000 clicks (20%), then we can be much more certain that it really is twice as good. Google doesn't trust us to calculate statistical significance without screwing it up somehow, so AdWords simply presents us with the answer and the Search Exam will only ask that we know what it is, not how it's determined.

The experiments feature doesn't need time to answer a question, it needs clicks. Even though Google has rules about how long experiments must run by time, it really doesn't matter. In the example at hand, if it takes 200,000 clicks to answer the question of which keyword performs best, then it makes no difference whether those clicks came pouring through in one morning or took an entire year. Either way, statistical significance is measured by the fact that enough clicks have taken place to be certain about the results.

When creating a new experiment, an advertiser must set an end date at least seven days away, but no more than 90. There could be a three day delay before a test of ad copy could begin because each variation must be approved. Once an experiment is underway, an advertiser can extend the end date or cancel it at any time with or without applying the experimental change to future traffic. Each experiment has a preset time to run and once time runs out, the changes will automatically go live by default.

If an experiment is nearing its end date and things are looking good, but have not yet passed the threshold of statistical significance, then you should probably extend it to get a statistically significant answer that can be acted on with confidence.

Bear in mind that statistical significance doesn't always identify what's important. It's possible to know with a high degree of certainty something that doesn't really matter all that much. If we're optimizing for conversions and learn from an experiment that one keyword consistently achieves a higher ad position, then so what?

CHAPTER 8: Overdelivery

The calendar we all use has 12 months of 28 to 31 days each, averaging 30.4 days. Google uses this average to calculate a monthly budget from a daily budget, and vice versa. The "budget" refers to a single campaign, not the total amount spent under the whole account. An advertiser might spend $350 per day overall across three campaigns which could have daily budgets of $200, $100, and $50 each. To find the three monthly budgets, multiply each daily budget by 30.4 to get $6,080, $3,040, and $1,520 respectively.

Let's say Fulano's Cuenca del Plata Travel sets their *cheap tickets* campaign's daily budget to $100 per day and all clicks cost $1.00. When the daily budget is reached, ads stop showing for that day and that advertiser gets no more AdWords traffic.

The monthly budget is $3,040 ($100 * 30.4) and if Google can provide exactly 3,040 clicks at $1.00 each, then that's how much they'll pay. If Google accidentally gave them more clicks, the bill for that campaign would still be for just $3,040 because that was the budget agreed to. If Google accidentally gave them fewer clicks, the bill for that campaign would be for however many were actually delivered. In such a case, Google would be leaving money out there that they could have captured if only they had been able to deliver 3,040 clicks that month.

Traffic Volume Fluctuations

To complicate things, search traffic volume fluctuates from day to day. Sometimes it's predictable (as in weekday versus weekend search patterns) and other times it's not (as when searches increase after a news event). Maybe airline ticket buyers try to game the system by purchasing tickets on the first or last day of the month, resulting in higher traffic on those days. Maybe there are riots reported in the news and interest in travel to a destination dips or a venue has been selected for an international sporting event so interest jumps.

The number of searches happening and the number of people interested in an offer are not consistent every day, so the number of clicks isn't consistent either. Maybe the highest traffic day of the month for the cheap tickets campaign brings 120 clicks at $120 while the lowest traffic day of that month brings 80 clicks for $80. The average would still be $100 per day.

To address this, Google will purposefully overdeliver on high-volume days by up to 20% *over* the daily budget (120% *of* the budget). They still aim to keep the monthly amount right at the limit set by the advertiser.

Although daily traffic fluctuates and there will be days when Fulano's Travel gets more clicks than they agreed to, at the end of the month they'll get what they wanted from Google: 3,040 total clicks for $3,040. Of course there's not one literal $80 day for every literal $120 day, but whatever number of clicks are overdelivered will other times be underdelivered to maintain the average. If Google's auto-magical system miscalculates and at month's end we see that 3,200 clicks happened, then the bill would still be for $3,040 because the surplus clicks would have been AdWords' fault.

Keep in mind that $120 is 20% *over* $100, but it's 120% *of* $100. When calculating the maximum overdelivery for a given day, we are multiplying by 120% (1.2) and not 20% (0.2). Any number larger than one is an increase in bidding and any number less than one is a decrease. An exam question about overdelivery could ask you to solve a problem requiring multiplication by a number over one, like using 1.2 instead of mistakenly using 0.2.

Purposeful Budget-Hopping Fluke

When *Clever Kevin* first learned of overdelivery, he hatched a plan and went looking for a business category where most orders happen during the first week of the month. His idea was to set a daily budget to $100 ($3,040/month) with the knowledge that so many conversions happen during the first seven days that AdWords would overdeliver $20 of clicks per day because the system expects to underdeliver later in the month. But at the end of that first week, he'll cancel his account without allowing it to run long enough to balance it out.

Would this scheme allow *Clever Kevin* to get $20 of free clicks every day for seven days? Nope. He would still owe $120 per day even though he set the daily budget to just $100. An exam answer will never involve black-hat budget manipulation or make it seem like AdWords settings can be gamed.

Accidental Budget-Hopping Fluke

The daily budget can be changed as often as wished at any time, and adjustments take effect immediately. A mid-day budget change can sometimes result in higher than expected spending on that day.

Let's say one of Fulano's Cuenca del Plata Travel's campaigns typically gets about 80% of all clicks before noon and 20% after. One day during lunchtime, Fulano changes that campaign's daily budget from $100 to $50. Before noon, probably $80 worth of clicks happened (80% of $100), the same as what would happen on any other morning. Then after noon (and after the change), there's still half a day so Google aims to spend half of the new $50 budget during that time ($25).

$80 before noon plus $25 after noon equals $105, which might be a surprise for Fulano who just slashed that campaign's $100-per-day budget in half. That might be unexpected, but it's in alignment with his instructions to AdWords for the first and second halves of that day.

CHAPTER 9: Conversion Tracking

One of the most indispensable tools of direct response efforts is *Conversion Tracking.* The exam is mostly concerned that you know what it is, why you want it, and can avoid the common pitfalls of installing it.

This Chapter covers a topic with an especially large gap between Examland and real world methods. When you read something here and think Google Analytics or some other solution is better than the tools within AdWords, you're probably right. This guide only covers what's relevant to the Search Exam.

There's a correlation between how amazing Google's services are and how much proprietary info you're willing to give them. If Google sends a user somewhere, then the only thing it knows is that the visitor walked in to that business' digital front door. Whether he bought anything and whether that click was worth paying more, less, or nothing for is a mystery without knowing what happened inside that digital store. Conversion Tracking is AdWords' way to follow visitor activity on your site to discover which traits high-value visitors have in common, and use that information to deliver more of them to you.

Among other uses, Conversion Tracking data reveals which keywords work best. We'd expect differences in conversion rates from people who arrived on our office cleaning client's website after searching for terms like *office cleaning, licensed office cleaning, bonded office cleaning, office cleaning free quote, janitorial cleaning service, janitorial cleaning free quote, facility maintenance service,* and *licensed and bonded facility maintenance.*

People searching for different terms will convert at different rates and the only way to know those rates is to run the keywords, pay for the clicks they generate, and then evaluate the Conversion Tracking data. Maybe we find out that people searching for *bonded office cleaning* make a purchase on our website twice as often as those who arrived after searching for *office cleaning free quote.* This is the kind of information used to reach direct response goals.

Installing Conversion Tracking

Almost all AdWords features involve operations that happen entirely inside the platform and are enabled or disabled by checking or unchecking boxes in the dashboard. Conversion Tracking is different because it needs information from the destination URL being advertised which requires us to do something outside of AdWords. It's accomplished by copy/pasting a snippet of code into the website which will send notification to AdWords whenever a conversion happens. The exam uses the terms "Conversion Tracking code," "tracking code," "code," and "snippet" interchangeably and I do too.

Google partially uses AdWords exams to train customers (like you and me) in processes where they constantly see things done incorrectly. One of those areas is the installation of tracking code and there are a few "don'ts" to cover. There are only two steps to tracking code installation: 1) get the code, and 2) paste it. In practice there's much more to it, but on the Fundamentals Exam, there's not.

Conversion Tracking Don'ts

To create a conversion tracking code, begin by clicking "+ Conversion" under the Conversions sub-tab in the Tools and Analysis tab. You'll be walked through the steps item-by-item until the last step when the system generates your custom tracking code and presents it to you for copy/pasting onto your site. In this process there are two steps that need special mention: The security level of the page served and the method used to notify users that you're tracking them.

The snippet works on both non-secure (http) and secure (https) pages, but only if you select the proper one during the code generation process. If a test question asks about an account for a site with secure pages that sees no incoming Conversion Tracking data, then an answer involving the installation of non-secure code should get your attention.

As far as Google is concerned, there are two options to notify users that a website uses Conversion Tracking, which brings us to the second issue. You can place the Google Site Stats Notification Box on your website by opting-in to it when generating the code. This option will show a visible box (that satisfies Google's specs) on your website. There is also the option to select "Don't add a notification" which assumes the advertiser will then write and publish his own notification, even if it's just an extra line in the site's privacy policy (that no one ever reads).

It looks like *Clever Kevin* just woke-up from his nap as it dawned on him that he could opt-out of the site stats box and then do nothing to notify users that he installed Conversion Tracking. How would Google ever know? Certainly he realizes Google sends a bot to skim his site for the presence of user notification language. If a test question involves opting-out of the site stats box, then the test answer will involve providing your own user notification language and no correct answer choice will ever assume it's OK to do neither. Any practice that is frowned upon by Google will not be part of a correct answer in Examland.

Where Tracking Code Belongs

Whenever someone buys something online, he sees a page immediately after the purchase is finalized which might say something like "Thank you for your order!" This only gets seen by someone who just ordered something and it's the exact page Conversion Tracking code should be installed on. Whenever the *Thank-You Page* loads and a user sees it, the installed code sends order-related info to AdWords. If AdWords sends a user to the site and no Conversion Tracking info was ever returned, then either the user never converted or something is wrong with the installation. It takes 24 hours after placing the snippet before the first statistics can be viewed.

A mistake is to place the code on the home page or in a template that gets used for all pages which would register a conversion every time anyone visits any page. It would be silly to write "Thanks for your order" on the landing page because the user hasn't ordered anything (yet) and that's the same rule to judge the appropriateness of tracking code. If a page can be seen by people who have not converted, then tracking code does not belong on it.

On those thank-you/conversion pages where tracking code does belong, the appropriate place is within the body tags. Even if web development isn't your responsibility and you've never seen a source file in your life, you still need to know that there are such things as body tags and in between them is the place for tracking code.

Web pages are presented as long text files and the body section contains commands for a browser about what to show and how to show it. The body section starts with a tag that reads <body> and it ends with another that reads </body>. These are far apart, nearly at opposite ends of the file (top and bottom) and the second one has a slash "/" to indicate the end of the body portion. Tracking code must go between them and Google suggests it goes immediately before the closing </body> tag.

Another mistake is placing the snippet inside footer or header information, or placing it in a template used for all pages. It does not matter if a website uses frames, pages are dynamically generated, written in PHP, or whatever other complication can be imagined. Just remember that tracking code always goes in between the body tags of a confirmation page.

Mobile Conversion Tracking

Mobile Conversion Tracking is an issue highly impacted by Enhanced Campaigns, which tries to track conversions across devices. Everything here is true both before and after the change to Enhanced Campaigns, which matters because some of the "current" test questions were born before Enhanced Campaigns existed. A big difference after the shift is that data about users can more seamlessly follow them from one device to another.

Just as it happens on a desktop computer, a conversion on a mobile phone is also marked by the serving of a thank-you page. But, *Click-to-Call* actions are an additional type of conversion to track on devices that can support phone calls. On high-end mobile devices (smart phones) any phone number that appears anywhere on the screen can be dialed by clicking it. But, only those which have mobile tracking code properly installed will record these actions as conversions.

Although they're almost identical and are created in the same way, a mobile tracking snippet is different than a regular one. This time when walking through the code generation process, you'd select *"Call on-site"* as the source. The bigger difference lies in the place where mobile code must be pasted.

A regular conversion happens whenever a thank-you page is served so we want to track when such a page appears on any screen on any device, and that regular thank-you page gets the regular code.

A click-to-call conversion happens whenever someone clicks a phone number so the mobile tracking snippet needs to be injected into the same line of code that contains the phone number, every place and every time it appears. This means the location of mobile tracking code is much more specific than just ensuring that it's pasted between body tags.

A phone number can be displayed as a text link, clickable image, or button, and the line of code that describes it is the exact place that needs the mobile tracking snippet. It's inserted as an *OnClick Command* to that line. Before the addition of the snippet, the line of code that contains the phone number might have effectively said something like "a button goes here, it says *Call Now,* and it's green." After the addition of the snippet, the same line would now effectively say "a button goes here, it says *Call Now,* it's green, and if someone clicks it then send a note to the AdWords system."

The action that mobile tracking code can monitor is when someone sees a number on his mobile phone screen, presses it, and the number is dialed by that same device. This doesn't mean that a sale has occurred, an appointment was set, or any of an advertiser's other end goals has happened. A click-to-call conversion is not a purchase conversion and they can't be compared.

CHAPTER 10: Search Funnels

Conversion Tracking provides more value when you can evaluate your Search Funnel to see the steps users take on their way to converting. The term *Search Funnel* is apparently the progeny of the term *Sales Funnel* which was never a perfect analogy.

Imagine a funnel used for pouring liquid into a container. Liquid enters the top and flows downward towards the spout where it exits. This is supposed to be a model of how Internet traffic flows, in which all of your advertising efforts are the funnel, users are the liquid, and the container at the bottom is full of those who converted.

If we have to stick with this analogy (and to deal with AdWords we do) then we have to admit we're most interested in the bottom of the funnel where the activity immediately before the conversion happens. We're inclined to focus more on the keywords (at the bottom of the funnel) that immediately precede conversions. We're less focused on what the user was doing last week (while still at the top of the funnel) when they were just starting to become interested in buying something and beginning to move through the process.

Conversion Paths

Our need to understand search funnels comes from the need to understand what *Search Funnel Reports* are. The reports show how users who eventually converted had interacted with our ads during their *Conversion Paths.*

Some keywords can be more responsible for introducing a user to your site and others can be more responsible for connecting the (now familiarized user) to a conversion. Google says you could "Think of these as different salespeople in a department store. One salesperson might be the person who first spoke to the customer, while another salesperson closed the deal."

A *Conversion Window* is the period between a first click and a conversion. To get an idea of how long it typically takes from the first click to the last, check the *Time Lag Report.* It's limited in that it can only report clicks on google.com, not the

Search or Display Networks. Still, it can be used to determine how long the window for your conversions typically is. The more commitment it takes to convert, the longer the conversion window. An email signup would likely have a shorter window than a $10,000 purchase. Users take longer when the risks of a bad decision are higher.

While on their conversion paths in the conversion window, users conduct multiple searches before finally converting. The metrics used in Search Funnel Reports reveal the value of the individual keywords that first got the ball rolling on a conversion.

The *Path Length* counts the average number of times visitors saw and/or clicked your ads before converting. Expect the majority to convert after one click, but don't be surprised to find there are many converters who saw or clicked your ads long before they finally converted.

An *Assisted Impression* is when a user's search triggers an ad impression which he does not click. The fact that a keyword has received impressions proves there has been early search activity which generated those impressions. If your reports show a large portion of converters saw your ad more than once before buying, then they have been doing a lot of searches that have triggered your ad. That indicates your product is something people buy after a lot of investigation.

An *Assisted Click* is generated when a user who clicks an ad lands on a site, but does not convert during the first visit. This visit could assist in a future conversion because he would be familiar with our site and would know about our product.

A *Last Click* is the click that most immediately preceded a conversion. A user who enters a branded keyword like your company's name is only searching for your product. The only way he knows to search for this is his previous introduction. That last click was immediately vital in the sale, but if there was any previous activity measured by these other indicators, then it gets some credit for its work in making this sale happen.

Moving Tracking Code

Let's look at the effect of moving tracking code between a post-conversion thank-you page and a pre-conversion point along a conversion path. We'll revisit the business model of María who was last seen running an auto sales lead generation operation in the Fundamentals Exam Prep Guide:

> On her site, there's a build-your-own-car game where a user can pick a current model car and swap colors, trim levels, and accessories until he has a shining 3D model of a car rotating on his computer screen. At the end of the game, he's presented with an offer: "Would you like to buy this exact car for real? Enter your info to get immediate quotes from local car dealers." A network of car dealers pays María $30 for each lead she gets.

María can place her code at any one of these steps. Conversion Tracking registers a conversion every time a page with the code loads without regard to why the page loads. She can place it on the page where the user initiates the game, the one where he completes the game, fills the form out, or the thank-you page he sees after he's completed the form. This is a funnel of ever-decreasing numbers, as not everyone who begins the game will finish and not everyone who finishes will fill-out the form. Let's say that on a given day there are 600 clicks to the site, 500 of them begin the game, 300 of those will actually finish, and then only three of those who finish will fill-out the form.

The conversion that's most directly correlated with María's business is the submission of a completed form, because that's the step when she makes money. The page where she'd likely place the tracking code is the one that reads "thanks for your info" but that thank-you page is only served to about three users per day.

If she had placed the tracking code on the previous page then she would have recorded 300 conversions and she would have had to use a different definition of what counts as a conversion. The reason she'd do that is if her conversion tracking was starved for data. She may be running 10,000 keywords and at a pace of just three full conversions a day, it'll take forever for her to find out the effectiveness of each one. If a low number of conversions just don't supply enough data to effectively optimize on, then María may have to track game completions instead of form-fills.

A warning needed here is not to compare data from a time when tracking code was at one step to another time when it was at a different step. It's also a bad idea to make other changes after moving the code and it should never be moved or removed when using the Conversion Optimizer (covered next).

If María previously lead AdWords to believe she'd pay $25 to produce a conversion (when a form gets filled which she can sell for $30) and AdWords continues to operate that way after she's moved the code, then the Google thinks she's willing to pay $25 for each game completion. That would ruin her campaign. If she wants to move the code, she needs to re-define the conversion value from the beginning as if there were no previous tracking data.

CHAPTER 11: Conversion Optimizer

Conversion Tracking is at the heart of the *Conversion Optimizer,* which won't even be an option without tracking. The Conversion Optimizer looks at past traffic patterns for variables that identify converters and then optimizes to send more of them.

Anyone considering using it would also have considered using the Enhanced CPC (ECPC) bidding model. Google says the difference is the Conversion Optimizer works better, while ECPC allows the advertiser more control. Like ECPC, the Conversion Optimizer uses Conversion Tracking data, optimizes for conversions, and adjusts the cost for each click accordingly. ECPC appears on the Fundamentals Exam while the Conversion Optimizer appears on the Search Exam, so each is covered in the relevant guide.

Two Bidding Models

The way to control the Conversion Optimizer is to raise or lower the CPA bid, just like adjusting a CPC bid is the way to control a CPC-based campaign. There are two ways to manage bids through the Conversion Optimizer.

The most familiar way is to set a *Max CPA* and pay an *Actual CPA.* This follows the precedent set during CPC bidding of setting the max as the most you'd pay, but then paying the smaller amount it takes to win an ad position higher than the next lowest bidder. As we'll see soon, the "max" isn't really the maximum you'll pay because sometimes the Conversion Optimizer delivers a CPA higher than what you set.

The other method is to set a *Target CPA* and then pay an *Average CPA.* Under this model, you'd set the Target CPA as what you'd like the Average CPA to be. Conversion Optimizer's challenge is to make that happen and deliver a number as close to that goal as possible, not higher and not lower. *Clever Kevin* wonders why anyone would want to ensure their CPA wouldn't go lower if the whole point is to get the lowest possible CPA. The CPA is still based on clicks and the same economics apply. If it's too low, your ads will never see the light of day.

Google recommends you leave all the arithmetic to them and set a Target CPA which they promise to adjust for.

Advertisers who don't quite trust Google to do whatever they want with no maximum threshold may be more comfortable setting a Max CPA. That's the big difference between the two approaches: Those who trust Google more can use the Target, and if those who trust them less can use the Max.

Under either model, Max and Target CPAs must be managed and the resulting Actual and Average CPAs must be analyzed. Lowering the one you set (max or target) would decrease the one you get (actual or average). It would also decrease traffic volume and the total number of conversions. Of course that means raising the one you set would increase the one you get, as well as increase traffic volume and the total number of conversions.

Rough Start

Conversion Optimizer is not for new campaigns or campaigns in which Conversion Tracking has just recently been implemented. The longer a campaign has had Conversion Tracking enabled, the better the Conversion Optimizer can be expected to work from the first day it's enabled. The more conversions have been recorded, the more accurate generalizations can be. Google advises us to begin using the optimizer with their recommended Max or Target CPAs and then adjust only after an initial period.

The minimums for time and clicks keep changing and they're different in different regions. Often, they are two weeks minimum time and 15 minimum clicks in the last 30 days. If a campaign were less than two weeks old, it's not eligible no matter how many clicks it has had. If it's a year old but has not had at least 15 clicks in the last 30 days, then it's not eligible no matter how old it is.

Google's help section on the Conversion Optimizer seems entirely dedicated to pre-emptively addressing the freak-out they anticipate someone could have when turning it on for the first time. They also want to inoculate us with an exam question or two against the stress rash we could get from not having our expectations properly set. It's important to Google that before we say the Conversion Optimizer isn't working, we define "working."

The metric that Google worries will spook us is the Conversion Rate. The purpose of the Conversion Optimizer is in the name: To optimize conversions. So we'd expect that of all goals, the Conversion Rate is the one that should increase and it should definitely not decrease. But sometimes, it does. A likely explanation for this is an influx of cheap clicks which have a slightly lower Conversion Rate at a seriously lower cost.

Let's see why that's good for the maker of a mobile app for weather info who has just turned the optimizer on. Our new client defines a conversion as an app download and before the Conversion Optimizer, they got 500 clicks per day at $1.00 each. Of those 500 visitors, 100 download the app giving them a Conversion Rate of 20%. Their CPA was $5. At the literal end of this representative day, they paid $500 for 100 downloads.

After enabling the Conversion Optimizer, they now get 1,000 clicks per day at an average of $0.50 (50 cents) each. Of those 1,000 visitors, 150 download the app so their Conversion Rate is only 15% which sets off an alarm because that's a steep drop form the 20% conversion rate they had before. But, their CPA this time is $3.33. More importantly, at the end of this day they paid $500 for 150 downloads.

In this example we saw the conversion rate go down, but we don't care. We've seen the CPA go down too and the raw number of conversions for the same budget went up, so the Conversion Optimizer worked.

Actual over Max

Now we get to a peculiarity that was foreshadowed a bit earlier. The Conversion Optimizer can be responsible for delivering an Actual CPA that exceeds the Max CPA. This most often happens with new campaigns in which it has been newly-enabled. Google hesitates to explain, other than to say that the optimizer is still figuring things out at first.

It can also happen when industries change, conditions within industries change, or seasonal shifts come and go. Let's say *Clever Kevin* has been hired by a new client who wants to generate leads for student loan consolidations. They run an especially profitable campaign which targets people with advanced degrees who work at non-profit organizations for high-interest, high-penalty loans. The Max CPA for a lead is $100 and they typically pay an Actual CPA of $90. Once the account is his to optimize, *Clever Kevin* immediately enables the Conversion Optimizer.

As always, the optimizer would use past tracking data to make adjustments oriented towards increasing future conversions. It can't adjust for changes in the environment that aren't evident in past data. If something about the environment is expected to change, then it could produce some poor results.

If the legal cap on exploitive interest rates for loans were changed from 25% to 24%, then the profitability of each new loan (and therefore the value per conversion) would go down in a way that the Conversion Optimizer wouldn't account for. If a new federal program launched that competed directly with this company's loan product, then the Conversion Optimizer's programmatic rules have no way of immediately adapting to this new reality. If a "student loan gate" story were to break in the news about the predatory practices of this company which effected demand, then the Conversion Optimizer won't understand why CTR and conversion rates decline.

When such shifts happen, this week's conversions would still be optimized based on last week's data which are no longer valid, possibly resulting in an Actual CPA higher than the Max CPA. Google goes out of its way to say there is no tool to predict performance and programmatic optimizations can only be made on pre-existing data.

After some time passes, the Conversion Optimizer will adapt to the new environment and begin to optimize for the new conditions. The CPA should come down over time and *Clever Kevin* should once again find the student loan consolidation business to be profitable. But the CPA can suffer temporarily, as long as the Conversion Optimizer is operating on old data that no longer apply.

Equivalent CPC

Even with the Conversion Optimizer working on a CPA basis, you're being billed by the click. AdWords determines the cost of clicks by establishing *Equivalent CPC Bids* which combine the Max or Target CPA we set and the conversion rate that the system predicts.

We'll walk through an outrageously simplified illustration with a client who offers online boating license courses. Their manual CPC campaign is set for $5 per click and on one sample day they get five clicks, which cost $25. These five clicks produce one conversion which is marked by a user enrolling in a course. Their conversion value is the profit from the course fee after expenses, which comes to $30. We'll represent this day's activity like this:

Click #1 - $5 = no conversion
Click #2 - $5 = one conversion
Click #3 - $5 = no conversion
Click #4 - $5 = no conversion
Click #5 - $5 = no conversion

One of these five visitors enrolls in a boating course so our client's CPA was $25 and if they made $30, then they're profitable. In summary:

The client spent $25
The client's CPA was $25
The client made $30
The client profited $5

Now let's see a representative day from later when the Conversion Optimizer has taken over. Even though it's focused on the CPA at the end, CPCs are still the currency that win ad impressions in auctions. Inside the Conversion Optimizer, these clicks are given a value as Equivalent CPC bids. Once those are all added up, the total dollar amount is what we owe Google.

For this example, it doesn't matter if we're using a Target or Max CPA. Let's imagine that either CPA is set for $25 to match the CPA we've been getting under the last plan we just left. We enable the optimizer and at the end of this next sample day they still got five clicks, but two conversions this time:

Click #1 - $9 = no conversion
Click #2 - $4 = no conversion
Click #3 - $18 = one conversion
Click #4 - $1 = no conversion
Click #5 - $8 = one conversion

All of those wild CPCs between $1 and $18 were decided by the optimizer inside of a black box that we don't really get to see. Our client spent more money on this day, but got two conversions.

The client spent $40
The client's CPA was $20
The client made $60
The client profited $20

This example is too simple, the numbers are too round and too far from realistic, and the variables aren't messy enough. But it just has to convey one point: The Conversion Optimizer optimizes for conversions, but you are still charged in good old fashioned clicks.

Compatibility

If a campaign runs on both the Search and Display Networks, then the Conversion Optimizer automatically adjusts bids on both and you can't set separate bids for one network or the other. You can only opt completely out of one.

All bid adjustments are ignored when the Conversion Optimizer is enabled (including Enhanced CPC). The lone exception is the -100% downward mobile adjustment which is the way to opt out of mobile traffic. It's unnecessary to do anything with old bid adjustment settings because they'll remain set (but ignored) so if you ever switch the Conversion Optimizer off, they'll be waiting to go back into effect. If an advertiser chose to return to CPC bidding after running the Conversion

Optimizer, then the campaign would also revert to the old CPCs that were in place previously.

Advanced ad scheduling is incompatible because it would allow you to adjust bids for different hours or days, which is the Conversion Optimizer's job. But, basic Ad Scheduling still works, so you can turn ads on or off for any hours or days you want. That means with the optimizer enabled, you cannot adjust a bid down -50% on the weekend, but you can turn it off completely for that same time period.

CHAPTER 12: Conversion Value

The whole reason for direct response advertising is to get conversions, whether that means an email submission for a blog, the purchase of a baby crib, a charitable donation, the completion of a how-to-pamper-your-cat game, or a phone call for Chinese food delivery. What's the most we'd pay for one of these to happen?

All Conversions vs. Unique Conversions

Some conversions only matter once per user and some matter every time the same user does them. If it's something like an email submission, then one user should count just once.

Remember María operates a lead generation website which hosts a form which captures the lead data she sells. Whether a user fills the form once or fills it with the same name and email address three times in a row, María gets just one user's info. Either way, the network of car dealers would pay her $30 per one user's lead information. In her business model, she would opt for *Unique Conversions* Tracking which only counts one conversion per user (for a 30 day period) no matter how many times the same user converts. Unique Conversions replaced the term *1-per-Click* tracking, which you may still find on an exam.

Whether María pays for one click or three is a separate question answered by the policies surrounding *Invalid Traffic* which gets its own chapter much later on.

The other option is *All Conversions* tracking (which replaced *Many-per-Click*) and counts a new conversion every time any user completes one for 30 days after an ad click (even if it's the same user over and over again). If María were selling car accessories online, then she would want to optimize even further for users who make many purchases because they're more valuable than those who buy only once. If a user makes two purchases, then All Conversions tracking will count two conversions as a result of the one ad the user encountered before arriving at María's site for the first time.

Once someone clicks an ad, Conversion Tracking will monitor his activity for that and future visits for a 30 day period.

If a user clicks an ad and visits a site today, then he returns to the site in 20 days (after some comparison shopping) to complete a purchase, then it counts. If he discovered the site through an ad, played the game but didn't fill-out a form on his first visit, then returned to play again and completed a form-fill 40 days later, then it doesn't count.

Value-per-Conversion

The *Value-per-Conversion* (VPC) is the amount of money it's worth to us to get one conversion. For the purchase of a baby crib, that's easy – how much is that one exact sale worth? For a Chinese food delivery phone call, it's tougher because not every call results in an order and each order is worth a different amount of money. For the completion of a how-to-pamper-your-cat game, it's subjective because a cat food advertiser has to judge what possible impact that would have on a user's likelihood to eventually purchase their brand in a store. By defining a VPC, an advertiser can know his upper bidding limit.

No one is more familiar than those at an agency with the fact that advertisers don't always understand the importance of advertising. Yet Google isn't fully convinced that agencies are able to convey to their clients the full impact of AdWords. They want people who would seek certification (you and me) to be impressed with the full value of proper advertising and know how to transfer this reverence to skeptical clients. In this way, test questions dealing with conversion value are looking to grade your ability to evangelize AdWords to others.

People with traditional media backgrounds will walk over familiar ground in this section. An advertiser who knows that one new customer can become a repeat customer would pay more to get one because he's not just paying to make one sale, but for all those future sales that could stem from the first. An advertiser who really believes he benefits from good word-of-mouth would pay more to get one customer because he believes this one will tell two friends who will then also become new customers. Those two new ones could in turn each tell two friends, who tell two friends... so the first sale is worth more because it results in all those other sales. Google believes in calculating *Word-of-Mouth Value* and *Lifetime Customer Value* (also known as *Repeat Business Value*), and these can show up on the test because (as Google says): "factoring in these values can give you the flexibility to bid higher."

Estimating Conversion Value

Today, we'll generate some leads for a Canadian wilderness summer camp. *Lead Generation* is when an advertiser is paying for a lead which may (or may not) turn into revenue. We're using AdWords to drive users to a landing page on the camp's website where we want them to submit their contact info through an online form. One of the camp employees can then call them on the phone and ask them to enroll their kid(s) for the upcoming summer. In this model, a conversion happens when someone fills-out a form and this example reveals the ways Google wants us to fully value it.

Short-Term Conversion Values are useful for maximizing short term growth and *Long Term Conversion Values* are useful for maximizing long term growth. Google wants the marketer (who they assume to be the one taking an AdWords exam) to be able to show his or her wilderness camp client that a large amount of money can justifiably be spent.

The short term conversion value is the most straight-forward. If our camp fee is $2,000 and 25% of that is profit, then each camper is worth $500. But many people who fill-out forms never send a camper, so if we get just one camper for every five form-fills, then each form-fill is worth just $100. That's it, calculation complete: We could pay a maximum of $100 per conversion because every fifth one results in a $500 profit.

Next Google wants us to factor word-of-mouth in to the conversion value. A new camper has a 50% chance of prompting the enrollment of a sibling or friend and for simplicity's sake, this camp offers no referral incentives.

There's one common mistake to be aware of that we already saw when we looked at overdelivery earlier. The lift of 50% is calculated as a gain so the actual number seen in an equation is 150% (or 1.50) and not 50% (or 0.50). So: $100 * 1.50 = $150. That first conversion was worth $100, but the word-of-mouth gain is 50%. We can pay up to $150 for a lead because 500 of them would probably bring us 100 campers and half of those 100 campers would bring a pal for an additional 50 enrollment fees attributed to good word-of-mouth.

We'll calculate lifetime customer value independently of the word-of-mouth example. Let's say campers, from the time they're old enough to attend wilderness camp until the time they're too old, attend an average of six summers. Some only come once and some come every summer for their entire childhoods, but six is the average at this camp.

Assuming prices never change, each student brings $500 profit per summer for six summers for total lifetime value of $3,000. If it still takes five leads to get one camper, then this camp could pay a max of $600 per lead. One summer's revenue of $2,000 multiplied by 0.25 (to isolate the profit portion of revenue), multiplied by 0.20 (to reduce for the one-in-five enrolment rate), multiplied by six summers equals $600. Considering only the Lifetime Customer Value while ignoring the word-of-mouth figure, $600 is the most that can be paid to acquire one new average camper.

Average Conversion Value

Now let's complicate our wilderness camp model even more. The details above only apply to the Standard Camp Program, which we project will account for 80% of the campers we'll get this summer. But there's also the Adventure Camp Program which includes off-site excursions.

If a visitor could convert in two different ways and we value them differently, then we need to know how much we could pay to get one visitor before knowing which conversion (if any) will happen. To determine that, we'll first determine the *Average Conversion Value*, which retailers like to call *Average Order Value* (AOV).

In a single campaign, we drive traffic to a single landing page with content about both camp programs. When a user fills-out the form, he must select which one he's interested in. For simplicity's sake, we'll say no user ever enrolls a camper for a program different than the one he initially inquired about and the same 1:5 ratio of form-fills turning into camp enrollments applies across both programs.

Our flagship Adventure Camp Program carries a $6,000 fee. If 30% of that is profit, then each camper is worth $1,800. Assuming the same 1:5 ratio of form-fills turning into campers, we could pay a maximum of $360 per conversion for those interested in Adventure Camp. We predict that 20% of all conversions will be from parents interested in this option.

The best info we have is: We're driving traffic to a site where 80% of our conversions are worth $100 and 20% are worth $360. Here's the formula for the most we can pay for an average conversion:

($VPC * % Conv. 1) + ($VPC * % Conv. 2) = Average VPC

To fill in our numbers from above, we get:

($100 * 0.80) + ($360 * 0.20) = Average VPC

Let's interpret. The first conversion type is worth $100 which is adjusted by the percentage of all conversions we expect will be that type. Then we get the result of adjusting the second conversion type's value of $360 by the 20% of all conversions we expect will be that type. Lastly, we add those two numbers together to get our answer, the Average Conversion Value. Let's start with Standard Summer Camp Program conversions:

($100)*(0.80) = $80

And do the same thing for Adventure Camp Program conversions:

($360)*(0.20) = $72

Lastly we add those two numbers together to get our Average Value-per-Conversion:

($80) + ($72) = $152

The results we expect to get for this campaign support us paying up to $152 for an average conversion. This is all based on our predictions of an 80/20 split between the two conversion types. If the actual results are that 85% go for the Standard

Camp Program and only 15% for the up-sell Adventure Camp Program, then this changes the inputs for the equation. Inputs also change if we find that only 1 in 8 Adventure Camp Program inquirers actually enroll (instead of 1 in 5), then the final Average Conversion Value would change too.

CHAPTER 13: More Keyword Management

In this chapter we'll cover the Keyword Planner, long-tail keywords, and keyword insertion.

Keyword Planner

The *Keyword Planner* is Google's tool for everything keyword-related. It supports our *Keyword Expansion* efforts to build the most expansive possible keyword lists because that raises the volume of activity on the platform, which often raises the amount of money we spend on AdWords. The planner gives ideas for new keywords, combines existing lists, recommends bids for keywords that we're not sure about, and shows how new ones could perform if they were live. An advertiser can get this information out of the tool by throwing other information in, like hand-typed starter keywords that describe what we're advertising, a landing page URL, an entire site's URL/domain, or by selecting pre-defined product categories.

This is an area where you might cross paths with an old holdout exam question that legend says is still served to test-takers periodically. In Examland, don't be surprised to see a question jump out of the bushes wearing an obsolete uniform while asking you to confirm that you know the Keyword Tool used to generate keyword lists. Its compatriot the Traffic Estimator used to give volume and cost estimates. In a revolution, the Keyword Planner replaced both.

Keyword Planner's Output

The Keyword Planner is set by default to show the whole universe of traffic available, which is almost never relevant to any one advertiser. To get more relevant estimates, it's necessary for us to apply the same settings in the Keyword Planner as we apply to our actual campaigns for location, language, and network selection.

Google wants you to do some exploring here and see how estimates change when you change or remove some of the restrictions. How much traffic are you missing out on because you're ignoring the Display Network? What if advertisers who target the US added Canada or those who target the UK added Ireland? How much bigger would your operation be if you simply checked one more box or opted-in to one more thing?

The Search Network Partners (non-Google sites that reserve space for AdWords search ads) have differing levels of acceptability for ads of different statuses. Some allow adult ads while some restrict AdWords to only showing kid-friendly ones. That means traffic estimates must consider these differences when estimating how many places an ad can show.

The Keyword Planner gives *Competition Estimates* as *Low, Medium,* or *High* which offer some level of insight into how many other advertisers are already bidding on a keyword and how much the CPCs are affected by their activity. Google won't say what the criteria are for these designations (like what "high" really means), so that won't be a test question.

Long Tail Keywords

One way to grow an existing campaign with the Keyword Planner is to find less-obvious *Long Tail Keywords*. The idea is to create a list of tens of thousands (or millions and millions) of less-popular keywords and assess their combined weight. Often the highest-converting keywords are the rarest and most oddly-specific ones.

Misunderstanding what "long tail" means is a common way for *Clever Kevin* to embarrass himself in front of someone who knows better. He reads blog posts advising him to try keywords with at least three words in them. He notices that pretty much all long tail keywords are composed of several words. As far as he's concerned, long tail = many words.

Picture a graph that lines up all of an account's keywords by frequency of search volume. The highest volumes on the left, and the lowest on the right:

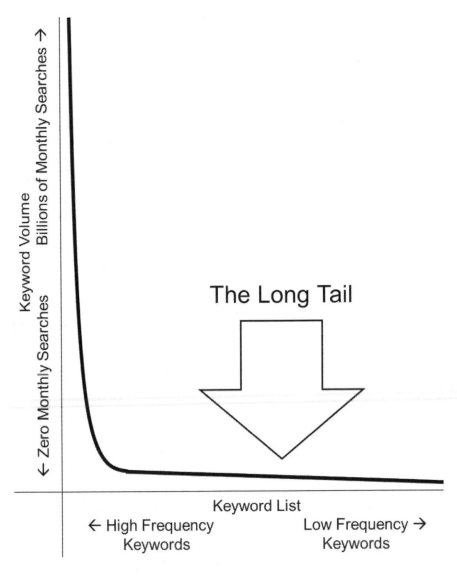

On the far left we might have the keyword *bike* which is searched for over 300,000 times per day, along with a few other select terms that are searched for at mind-boggling frequencies. After those first few superstars, the volumes take a nose dive and we see something like *cruiser bike* which is searched for 9,000 times per day. Even though its volume is just 3% of *bike*, it still might be in the top 10 of all keywords, just nine spaces back. Then way further down in volume (and way further to the right) we see a keyword like *58cm aluminum men's drop bar 26" road bike 21 speed* which has had few searches ever.

Something like a specific product name or model number might be millions of places from the top in search volume, as almost no one is typing that exact term into google.com. If you graphed this distribution, you'd see a super high peak on the far left where our precious few superstar keywords live and then a steep drop-off that leads down to our low volume words. If we keep following it left, we'd see a long line that just hovers a little above zero as it stretches to the right for millions and millions of oddball keywords that are seldom searched for. That line is called the long tail and those keywords are long tail keywords.

In the real world, the long tail gets cropped. This is all a thought experiment as Google would likely give such a specific keyword the status of *Low Search Volume,* which makes it inactive for having too few searches. Although Google publically endorses the strategy and using it is the right answer in Examland, their policy keeps us from pursuing it very far in the real world.

The problem with long tail keywords is they're hard to manage. There are so many and each one has such a low volume that it's hard to justify spending too much of your day to perfect a keyword that (if you dominated it) might get you two visits a year.

The power of long tail keywords is that they often convert at the highest rates. A user searching for *bike* might click an ad and be interested in the cruiser bike advertised, but a user searching for *cruiser bike* is more interested and more likely to buy. And then there's the user searching for *58cm aluminum men's drop bar 26" road bike 21 speed,* who is demonstrating the highest possible intent. He's probably going to buy that exact item in the next few minutes and if you sell such a thing, you want your ad in front of him right now.

The Keyword Planner is supposed to help you identify keywords like this. It's necessary to review each one it generates because it's an automated process that produces some puzzling suggestions that have nothing to do with what you advertise.

Keyword Insertion

Keyword Insertion (also called *Dynamic Keyword Insertion* (DKI)) involves designating space in an ad for the search term that triggered it. An advertiser could specify the keywords *mountain bikes, road bikes, BMX bikes, fixed bikes, cruiser bikes,* and *recumbent bikes* with ad copy that reads "Save on _____." Then if the user's search term included *mountain bikes,* the ad would read:

Save on **Mountain Bikes**
www.example.com/**mountain-bikes**
Professional **Mountain Bikes**
No tax plus free shipping

Notice how we can incorporate the search term into the headline, description lines, and display URL. If a user search contained *road bikes,* the ad would read:

Save on **Road Bikes**
www.example.com/**road-bikes**
Professional **Road Bikes**
No tax plus free shipping

As always, whenever a user's search term matches one in the copy of an ad, the term will appear **bold** in the ad.

This can make an ad more relevant to users because someone whose search included *BMX bikes* is more apt to be receptive to an ad that uses the same phrase. Because of the expected increase in relevancy, it's also expected that CTR will rise.

An ad triggered by a broad match will still show the advertiser's chosen keyword in the ad that's served, instead of the user's complete search query. Let's say a user searches for *off road bikes* which triggers the broad match keyword *road bikes.* The actual ad that AdWords generates would still read "Save on **road bikes**" just like before.

The full phrase *off road bikes* wouldn't show in the ad copy because it was not the advertiser's chosen keyword that's responsible for triggering this ad. Imagine the result if a user who typed a curse word followed by the term *road bikes* saw your ad which read:

Save on $@%# Road Bikes
www.example.com/$@%#-road-bikes
Professional **$@%# Road Bikes**
No tax plus free shipping

Memorize this for the exam: **{keyword:default text}**. The way to employ Keyword Insertion is to slip that funky punctuation directly into the ad copy which is how to instruct AdWords to replace those marks with terms from the user's search query. Google literature calls this code, but it's just one syntactical colon between two curly brackets.

The "default text" portion of {keyword:default text} is a placeholder for the text that shows when your ad is served without an inserted keyword. If we used {keyword:Bike Styles} and the ad were served without a user term inserted, it would read:

Save on Bike Styles
www.example.com/
Professional Bike Styles
No tax plus free shipping

One reason why an ad would show with the default text instead of the user's search term inserted is because the chosen keyword would create ad copy that's over the character limits. It's always true that the headline can be no longer than 25 characters and each description line has a max of 35 characters (including spaces). It doesn't matter if ad copy came into existence through Keyword Insertion or any other method. If it's too long, then it's un-runnable. This ad could never show:

Save on **Fixed Gear Aluminum-Framed Bicycles**
www.example.com/ **fixed-gear-aluminum-framed-bicycles**
Professional **Fixed Gear Aluminum-Framed Bicycles**
No tax plus free shipping

Keyword Insertion works with any text portion of any text ad, including extensions. Before running any, find out what the end result actually looks like by using the Ad Preview and Diagnosis Tool.

Sloppy Copy

Clever Kevin shouldn't get carried away with the lighting strike of an idea that he could craft an ad so that the blank could be filled with absolutely anything to drive massive traffic to his site, like:

Buy _____ at 90% off
ringtonesbycleverkevin.com/
We Have Everything in
The World in One Place!

The exam may check to see that you know this won't work and would embarrass you if it did. There's something wrong with each of these following examples, beginning with the fact that motorcycles don't have steering wheels:

Steering Wheels in Stock
example.com/**steering-wheels**
Thousands of **Steering Wheels**
for Cars, Trucks, and Motorcycles

Wholesale **Elders**
example.com/
Fantastic Prices on **Elders**
Always Free Shipping!

Furniture por Mayor
ejemplo.com/**furniture**
Precios Fantásticos en **Furniture**
Siempre Envio Gratis!

Looking for **Human Heads**?
example.com/
Find Exactly what you Want.
Search Millions of Products.

Discount Flights to **Hell**
example.com/**hell**
Why not get-away to **Hell**?
Cheap flight, book tonight!

Up to 82% off of {keyword}
example.com/
Biggest {keyword} Warehouse!
Licensed {keyword} Dealer

Online auction and shopping websites are infamous for creating some excruciatingly bad ads through the poor execution of Keyword Insertion. To see some more "do nots," enter *keyword insertion fail* into your favorite search engine and the results will yield plentiful examples of how it can all go wrong.

Ad Copy Policy & DKI

You *can* use purposefully-misspelled words, curse words, trademarked words, your competitor's name, or just about anything else as keywords and if a user searches them, your ad can appear. But when the ad does appear, AdWords policy prohibits those same kinds of terms from appearing in the ad copy, no matter how they got there. The implication for Keyword Insertion is that any term that can't be in an ad's text can't be used as an inserted keyword. The ways DKI can be used are limited by the limits placed on ad copy.

Any policy-violating ad that *Clever Kevin* can imagine creating through the novel use of Keyword Insertion is still subject to the same policies as everything else. If an ad built for Keyword Insertion is crafted so sloppily that the result is gibberish, then it'll be a dis-approvable ad and probably won't be awarded a status which allows it to run. Google also recommends avoiding the use of any special characters that aren't supported by all browsers. The cuter you get, the higher the chance that the user would see gibberish.

CHAPTER 14: Dynamic Search Ads

A large e-commerce retailer with millions of products in need of millions of ads can save an awful lot of time with *Dynamic Search Ads* (DSAs). The exam doesn't have any questions that are meant for someone responsible for such an operation, but Google does expect you to at least know that using Dynamic Search Ads saves time. This is especially true for sites that sell a large variety of frequently changing items or an ever-changing roster of seasonal items.

Dynamic Search Ads are a keyword-less ad type. AdWords scans the content of the site being advertised to determine what kinds of search terms should trigger ads for which products. It does this using Google's organic search index to determine which searches are relevant to it.

The moment your DSA is triggered, AdWords instantly generates a new ad with a customized headline and a destination URL that links directly to the page on your site that's most matched to the user's search query. Within that moment, the headline is stitched-together dynamically with terms from both the search query and the site content. The description and display URL are a template that's been premade by the advertiser.

When to Use Them

Dynamic Search Ads exists so an advertiser who is unable to dedicate the time needed to manage keywords for the least profitable or lowest volume products can simply put them on an AdWords program that's "good enough." Imagine applying "the 80/20 rule" to this. If 20% of products return 80% of sales and the other 80% are only responsible for 20% of sales, then those least active 80% are good candidates for DSAs. This ad type is for the slowest moving inventory that you don't have time to deal with.

Dynamic Search Ads exist to capture the traffic that's not already being targeted by keywords. Google expects that a campaign triggered by DSAs will yield more traffic than one in which only pre-selected keywords are in play. But because they're not as finely crafted and not as much effort goes into each one, it's expected that DSAs won't work as well as regular keyword-targeted ads.

Another reason why it could still be worthwhile to employ DSAs is to generate keyword research data. AdWords keeps a log of all the DSAs that get clicks and the user searches that triggered them. The Search Terms Report presents you with these search terms which should probably be added as keywords to ensure that you continue to capture that traffic.

Description Lines

Because we'll need to pre-write the description lines without knowing exactly which of our products they'll advertise, descriptions should apply widely across the whole site. We can promote "Free shipping on orders over $25," "Buy one get one free," or "20% off with code SEARCHCERTS." Brand messages that cover the entire company, site-wide promotions, or discounts are all fitting messages. Let's bring all this together in a few examples of how finished ads might look:

Hex Jam Lock Nuts
example.com/nuts
Free shipping on
orders over $25!

Zinc Plated Bolts
example.com/bolts
Free shipping on
orders over $25!

High Collar Washers
example.com/washers
Free shipping on
orders over $25!

Of course example.com/nuts is only the display URL which would direct users to the destination URL that might look more like example.com/products/fasteners/nuts/hex/78jet36dhh.

When Not to Use Them

Websites that don't sell a large variety of products and those focused on comparisons, ratings, reviews, affiliate sales sites and sites that sell customized gifts are all unfit for Dynamic Search Ads. There are keywords that Google could skim from an advertiser's product pages that it would have trouble matching to user queries. Imagine that the titles of products in an online store are:

Boston Terrier cell phone case

Boston Terrier sweater

Boston University dog sweater

Maybe a human knows that a search for *Boston Terrier cell phone case* should return ads for cell phone cases that feature images of Boston Terriers, but AdWords might not be able to tell and serve ads related to either Boston Terriers or cell phones.

Before we decide that humans always know better, consider the others. Should a search for *Boston Terrier sweater* return ads for a sweater depicting Boston Terriers or a dog sweater that would be worn by a Boston Terrier? The Boston Terrier is the mascot of Boston University. Should a search for *Boston University dog sweater* return ads for a sweater featuring the Boston University mascot? Or for a sweater worn by a dog that features the Boston University logo? If we can't tell, then AdWords can't tell and this kind of product shouldn't have anything to do with Dynamic Search Ads.

Dynamic Ad Targets

Advertisers who should use Dynamic Search Ads match their products to user searches by creating *Dynamic Ad Targets* (also called *Auto Targets*). This serves the same purpose for DSAs as building keyword lists serves for regular campaigns and there are five ways to do it.

The first Dynamic Ad Target is *All Webpages* which will activate DSAs for every page of an entire domain (the whole site) even non-product pages.

Dynamic Ad Targets can also be created by selecting pre-defined *Categories,* in the same way a user would browse your e-commerce site by category and sub-category. This is the kind of thing that's applied to parts of a website, there's no expectation that the whole domain can be described with one category. You can assign sections to categories like "fasteners," "pneumatics," or "hydraulics." You can also create your own categories but Google advises against this because AdWords might not know what your category name means and therefore can't match it to anything.

You can also designate Dynamic Ad Targets by designating content via keywords. Any page of your site where those words are found is a page marked as a Dynamic Ad Target. The words *bolts* and *washers* can be chosen for example. This is like applying content targeting measures to your own site instead of to a Display Partner site.

The fourth way you can create a Dynamic Ad Target is by identifying URL strings that your advertise-able pages have in common. Let's say your pages all fall under these directories:

example.com/products
example.com/services
example.com/about
example.com/contact
example.com/locations

In this case, it's probably most useful to specify any URL which includes *products* as a Dynamic Ad Target. AdWords would match ads for any URL with the word *products*. Take a moment to actually read (and not glaze past) these examples:

example.com/**products**/fasteners/bolts/yu78g7bf8c
example.com/**products**/pneumatics/compressors/m64re4h8n4
example.com/**products**/hydraulics/filtration/k22j2df3r7

Specifying *products* as a word that must appear in URL strings would not match ads for other pages under that domain which don't include it, like:

example.com/about/team/president
example.com/services/hjn09s7d5w
example.com/contact/main

Maybe some of our larger products in the pneumatics and hydraulics sections are worth the time needed to manage keyword-targeted campaigns, so we just want to set Dynamic Ad Targets for the thousands of tiny products like those in the fasteners category. We'll tell AdWords to match ads for any URL with the word *fasteners*, like:

example.com/products/**fasteners**/nuts/yu78g7bf8c
example.com/products/**fasteners**/bolts/m64re4h8n4
example.com/products/**fasteners**/washers/k22j2df3r7

Dynamic Ad Targets can also be created via the fifth and final method by designating page titles for inclusion. This shares the same strategy as the last method, it's just a matter of how your directories are organized that would dictate which of these does a better job of identifying the products you want to set Dynamic Ad Targets for. Any page that includes the given lines can be included, like:

<title> Nuts </title>
<title> Bolts </title>
<title> Washers </title>

Any of the methods we've just reviewed for creating Dynamic Ad Targets can also be used to designate pages to *exclude* from the campaign. Google urges advertisers to create exclusions for pages containing terms like *out of stock, sold out, unavailable,* or whatever other terms that advertisers' site uses for product pages that aren't currently active. It's also a good idea to exclude some static portions of the site that don't have anything for sale like the *blog, privacy policy,* or *career* sections.

Negative keywords also apply to DSA campaigns in the exact same way as any other campaign and will prevent the serving of an ad for queries that include those terms. The difference is that exclusions keep Dynamic Ad Targets from being created for a page while negatives keep the ad from showing when the terms are in a query.

CHAPTER 15: Product Listing Ads

Neither the Dynamic Search Ads we've seen in the last chapter nor *Product Listing Ads* (PLAs) use keywords, and both are suited for the same kinds of huge e-commerce advertisers. Product Listing Ads stand on their own (they're not extensions) and pull information directly from the Google Merchant Center Feed, which is the connection between an AdWords account and a Google Merchant Center account. The advertiser controls this process by managing Product Targets, which we'll cover at the end of this chapter.

Unlike Any Other Search Ad Type

PLAs can show on regular google.com results pages and on Google Shopping results pages. Unlike regular search ads, they're presented as tall rectangles with an image, headline, price and the name of the advertiser. That's usually all that shows and they're remarkable for serving an image in response to a user search. A user who searches for *50 gallon per minute hydraulic filter* may see a PLA that only reads "ABC Brand 50gpm Hydraulic Filter $299 ExamleCo1.com." The focus of that short ad is a product image:

A Product Listing Ad is image-centered and their most salient feature is a hero shot of the product. The *Hero Shot* is an image of the product looking as appealing as it possibly can, like a hero that's swooped in to answer the user's question. The job of telling users where the ad will take them is done by the company name, instead of the usual display URL. The name is not set in AdWords, but inside the linked Merchant Center account.

The job of the description lines in a regular ad is often left undone, but when it is done, it's the *Promotion* (sometimes called *Promotional Message*) that does it. Promotions are the final Product Listing Ad element, after image, headline, price, and company name. They're optional messages that convey a selling proposition that's relevant to the entire ad group in 45 or fewer characters:

Ads

ABC Brand 50gpm
Hydraulic Filter
$299 - ExampleCo1.com
Free shipping on orders
over $25

XYZ Brand 50gpm
Hydraulic Filter
$279 - ExampleCo2.com
Buy one get one free

Acme Brand 50gpm
Hydraulic Filter
$199 - ExampleCo3.com
20% off with code
SEARCHCERTS

In the same spirit as the description lines of Dynamic Search Ads in the last chapter, PLA promotions are messages like "Free shipping on orders over $25," "Buy one get one free," or "20% off with code SEARCHCERTS." They're not specific to just one individual product, but apply to everything in an ad group. If one says "Buy one get one free," then that should be true for every product in that ad group.

PLA Practices

When we employ PLAs, Google encourages us to break their "only one of your ads per search results page" rule. One user query can trigger more than one PLA from the same advertiser, in addition to one regular text ad (in addition to any organic results). With Product Listing Ads, your ads can appear on more of *Page One* than Google would otherwise allow.

Only Manual CPC or CPA bidding models are compatible with Product Listing Ads. Many advertisers begin the transition to PLAs with the same Max CPC or Max CPA as their regular keyword-targeted campaigns, but then optimize bids separately from there.

Product Listing Ad conversion rates are typically higher than those of regular text ads. This can partially be explained by the fact that price and product info are in the PLA ad copy, so anyone who clicks is qualifying herself as someone who wants the product and accepts the price.

For those advertisers who also have physical retail locations, Google's best practices are to increase bids for mobile devices and increase them for users who are physically located in or near our location(s). Anyone who's shopping the isles of our store should see our Product Listing Ad. Whether she's researching an in-store purchase on her phone or researching an online purchase in our store, we want her buying from us.

Product Targets

We must set *Product Targets* to control which products are eligible to show in PLAs. Our Merchant Center Feed must be current and its information accurate. It can be updated four times per day at the most.

Product targets have to match what's already present in our Merchant Center account. We can't tell AdWords to advertise something we don't sell and as far as Google is concerned, our Merchant Center includes everything we've got to sell.

When we connect Merchant Center and AdWords accounts, all products in out Merchant Center will automatically be opted-in to PLAs. The way to control this is through the use of filters to keep out certain types of products in the feed. Filters tell AdWords what *not* to advertise.

CHAPTER 16: Location Extensions

Location Extensions are suited to advertisers with physical locations who can add addresses, phone numbers, and maps to otherwise plain text ads.

Location Extensions are served only to users who are within the area the advertiser specifies (as opposed to those outside who show interest in the area). There are two types of geographic targeting. *User Location* targeting is meant to reach people who are physically located in a named area. *Locations of Interest* targeting is meant to reach users who are not there, but are interested in the place. A user in Delhi who searches for *seafood cuisine in Delhi* or *Delhi seafood cuisine* would see user location-targeted ads, while a user in Mumbai who searches for the same term would see ads targeted by location of interest.

Location Extensions can show on google.com and the Search Network, and most prominently on Google Maps. Within Google Maps there's a left panel for search results which can include *Map Markers* (those little red pushpin symbols) that show paid Location Extension info.

Ads with high enough bids and Quality Scores can appear with Location Extensions that show multiple addresses. But, they're easily overridden by other kinds of extensions that could show instead. If an ad has more than one extension attached to it, then a Location Extension would likely be the one that does *not* show.

Discoverability

When the names of physical places are used as keywords, AdWords will match them as variants of each other, such as *New York, New York City, NY,* and *NYC.*

Let's say Amuk Seafood Grill is a huge single location restaurant in Delhi, India. We'll include *seafood cuisine* as a phrase match keyword, so other terms (like *Delhi*) can appear before or after it. When a user searches *Delhi seafood cuisine, seafood cuisine in Delhi,* or *top seafood cuisine Delhi*, Amuk's ad can show with a Location Extension to users who are physically located in or near Delhi:

Amuk Seafood Grill
www.example.com/greater-kailash
The Freshest Cuisine
and Exceptional Quality
Amuk Enclave
Greater Kailash
New Delhi, Delhi 110048
011 1234 5678

If the imaginary Amuk Seafood Grill is in the Greater Kailash district of Delhi, then Google's best practice is to add the term *Greater Kailash* to the keyword list. When location is so important to a business (as it is with restaurants) it should be included in the ad copy too. To increase this ad's relevancy to the user, any keyword that's specific enough to trigger an ad can also be used in the ad itself:

Amuk Seafood Grill
www.example.com/greater-kailash
The Freshest Cuisine
in Greater Kailash
Amuk Enclave
Greater Kailash
New Delhi, Delhi 110048
011 1234 5678

Remember that when a user's search terms, our keywords, and our ad copy all match, they'll appear in **bold**. When a user who's physically located in the area searches for *Greater Kailash seafood cuisine*, this ad is more likely to get his attention:

Amuk **Seafood** Grill
www.example.com/**greater-kailash**
The Freshest **Cuisine**
in **Greater Kailash**
Amuk Enclave
Greater Kailash
New Delhi, Delhi 110048
011 1234 5678

Campaign vs. Ad Group Level

By default, Location Extensions are assumed to apply to an entire campaign with the idea that any advertiser they're appropriate for will only be concerned with the region they define in their location targeting (which is set at the campaign level). Campaign level Location Extensions take less time to manage than those set at the ad group level. The limitation is they require running the same exact ad copy and landing page for all locations.

With ad group-level Location Extensions, an advertiser can run unique ad copy and an individual landing page for each location. The downsides are they take more effort to set up and any ad under an ad group-level Location Extension will not show for any search in which the user did not use a location-related term.

Location Insertion

Location Insertion works similarly to Keyword Insertion (covered earlier) in which curly brackets { } are used to designate a "fill-in-the-blank" portion of ad copy which gets populated as the ad is served. Instead of keywords, this time ad copy can be customized to the user by city, postal code, and/or phone number.

If I can interject a personal story for a moment, while working at a company that sold local advertising, I once received a misguided call from a florist who thought my phone number was a complaint line for things he didn't like about the Internet. That day I learned Location Insertion might be the AdWords feature local florists understand the least and despise the most because it allows a national floral company to fake localness from afar. They can run ads that read:

Loamshire Florist
example.com/ **999-123-4567**
A beautiful bouquet today
55555 Main Street, **Loamshire**

Local Loamshire florists might not know what Location Insertion is, but they know they don't like it one bit. It allows ads to include the local area name and a local phone number (in this case we're imagining that "999" is a legitimate area code).

Google Places

Google Places accounts are only for business owners and it's against Google policy for a search engine marketer to possess such an account. There's no good reason for this topic to be on an exam intended for marketers, but it is. We'll cover it to the extent that it's on the test.

Google Places is for owners of physical brick-and-mortar stores to list their locations in Google Maps to become more visible in organic local search results. It's a way for Google to crowd-source its info gathering by allowing these owners to self-report basic facts about their businesses. Google Places info can also be used for paid campaigns even though its main purpose is to aid the accuracy of organic results.

Once a Google Places account holder links it to their AdWords account, her *Business Listing(s)* (physical address(es)) will be applied to all campaigns. Adding or updating business listings in Google Places will automatically update addresses in the ads of a linked AdWords account.

Let's say one company owns both Amuk Seafood Grill and Amuk Eyeglass Superstore. If they simply linked their Google Places and AdWords accounts, then the locations of both brands would be connected to all ads in the AdWords account. This needs to be fixed by filtering Amuk Seafood Grill in and filtering Amuk Eyeglass Superstore out. If there's a central headquarters office for Amuk Seafood Grill, it would also be filtered out because it is not a restaurant location where we want hungry people coming for a meal. If Amuk has a separate campaign for advertising employment opportunities and they want prospective employees to contact their headquarters office (instead of applying directly to individual restaurant locations), then those restaurant locations would be filtered out of that campaign.

Mobile Location vs. Call Extensions

Call Extensions (you might know them as the *Click-to-Call* function) are separate from Location Extensions, but covered in this chapter because there's so much overlap with *Mobile Location Extensions*. Both allow users on mobile devices to call an advertiser's phone number directly from an ad on a *High-End Mobile Device* (smart phone) and any other device that can both browse the Internet and place a phone call.

Call Extensions and Mobile Location Extensions are both tied to the place and time a user is presented an ad, they both include phone numbers, and they're both situations when the user is able to keep his buying activity offline. You can also schedule both to show only during hours and days when someone will be available to answer the phone. In account statistics, even if no one is calling, Google hopes you'll notice CTR for standard browser clicks is probably higher for an ad with a phone number than without.

A business that has one national phone number which all users should call is best served with Call Extensions while a business that has many locations which each have different phone numbers which users should call is best served by Mobile Location Extensions. Naturally, Google suggests enabling both kinds.

Let's say Amuk Seafood Grill is now a chain of 100 locations across India. A Mobile Location Extension would direct a user to the one location (of those 100) that he is physically closest to, so that's appropriate when encouraging users to call for dinner reservations. A Call Extension would show all mobile users the same phone number no matter where they are. Amuk Seafood Grill might find this useful if they were adverting for employment and wanted prospective employees to first call their human resources department at a single national headquarters office.

A Mobile Location Extension looks almost exactly like a regular Location Extension, with the addition of a small *Directions* link for devices that have not opted-out of sharing their location data:

Amuk Seafood Grill
www.example.com/greater-kailash
The Freshest Cuisine
in Greater Kailash
Amuk Enclave
Greater Kailash
New Delhi, Delhi 110048
011 1234 5678 - Directions

A Call Extension shows on regular ads without an address (and often without any other extension) and simply posts a "call" button next to the ad:

Jobs at Amuk, Inc.
www.example.com/careers
Join the top of the
Hospitality Industry.

Call Metrics Reporting (usually known as just *Call Reporting*) provides data on a call's duration, device that placed it, and the usual PPC metrics as applied to phone calls. Google records these details through a *Google Forwarding Number* and that can only be used with Call Extensions.

CHAPTER 17: More Ad Extensions & Annotations

Anyone who's passed the Fundamentals Exam should have some familiarity with *Ad Extensions*. Google decides which extensions to show with an ad based on what combination of ad and extension it predicts would perform the best. They don't cost anything, but clicks do and the advertiser pays the same amount for a click on any part of the ad or extension.

Google insists that we should always employ all applicable extensions to all campaigns. The only time one should not be employed is when it's not suited to the type of campaign in use. Big factors of which ads show extensions are relevance, ad position, and available space. The ways we can increase the showing of extensions are to increase bids, Quality Score, or both in pursuit of better ad position. It also doesn't hurt to tighten ad groups to raise the relevance between keywords and ads. In this chapter we'll cover several extension types.

Seller Ratings Extensions

Advertisers are sellers, and Seller Ratings rate them. Users who are presented with *Seller Ratings Extensions* can compare them when deciding which ad to click and/or open the extension to further read specific reviews.

Ratings are about the user's experience with the business, not the products they bought and they're matched to a seller based on the domain of the destination URL. If a user bought a one-star space heater from a five-star seller, then the rating should be five stars. If she bought a four star space heater from a two-star seller, then it should be two stars.

These extensions are mostly for products, but service providers are also rated. To be eligible, a seller must have had at least 30 unique reviews in the last 12 months with an average rating of at least 3.5 stars. A one-star business won't be penalized by having their one-star appear in the extension to warn shoppers about how lousy they are.

The star rating is visually represented by little five-point star symbols in front of text that gives the number of seller reviews:

Loamshire Florist
example.com/ 999-123-4567
★★★★★ 41 seller reviews
A beautiful bouquet today

Portable Space Heaters
★★★★★ 9,448 seller reviews
example.com/
Brand Names on Sale!

Seller Ratings Extensions are not something that advertisers create or optimize and the exam won't ask you how to manage things that Google won't allow you to manage. It can ask that you know what they are, so that's all we're covering here.

Any advertiser meeting Google's criteria for Seller Rating Extensions will automatically be eligible for them, even though they took no action to initiate this. Google says it aggregates ratings submitted by users of their services (especially Google Shopping and Wallet) and third-party sites that have formal agreements with Google. The only way to opt-out is through a form.

Often Google's advice is dismissive and ignores the realities faced by marketers and advertisers but in this instance, I enthusiastically echo their advice for those worried about a low rating: "The best way to improve your ratings is to make sure that your customers receive excellent customer service." Be a better seller.

Sitelinks

Sitelinks are extensions that show the most popular pages on a site so that clicking one will direct a user to that destination within the advertiser's domain instead of the ad's designated destination URL. Google expects ads with Sitelinks to have higher overall CTR, in part because users are presented with more than one thing to click on.

Sitelinks can be set for a campaign or ad group and by default, all ad groups in a campaign will show that campaign's Sitelinks. If one is set for an individual ad group, then it overrides the campaign level setting. You can apply Ad

Scheduling settings to run (or exclude from running) Sitelinks during the days or hours you choose.

Just like Google encourages newer AdWords advertisers to structure their accounts by mirroring the structure of their website, the same is true for Sitelink ideas. To choose which pages of a site should get their own Sitelinks, look at those which are suitable as points of first time entry.

You can (and Google wants you to) create a pool of 10 Sitelinks per campaign. Ads shown on computers can show 2-6 Sitelinks, 2-4 on smart phones, and none on *WAP* (non-smart) phones. The text submitted for Sitelinks (sometimes called *Link Text*) should be short to maximize the number that can show. Longer copy for each one means that fewer can show. There's a limit of 25 characters total.

An ad can show on a mobile device with four Sitelinks and full link text:

Amuk Seafood Grill
www.example.com/greater-kailash
The Freshest Cuisine
in Greater Kailash

Restaurant Locator
Find an Amuk Seafood Grill
in your neighborhood.

Seasonal Specials
The freshest seafood is
Always in season!

Menu
See our delicious selection.

Gift Cards
Know a seafood lover with
an upcoming birthday?

Or that same ad could show the same four Sitelinks without link text:

Amuk Seafood Grill
www.example.com/greater-kailash
The Freshest Cuisine
in Greater Kailash

Restaurant Locator

Seasonal Specials

Menu

Gift Cards

And of course it could show with only two Sitelinks:

Amuk Seafood Grill
www.example.com/greater-kailash
The Freshest Cuisine
in Greater Kailash

Restaurant Locator

Seasonal Specials

When an ad is served, AdWords decides how many of which Sitelinks to show and what their order should be for that particular ad impression. The next time the same one shows, the selection, number, and sequence of Sitelinks (or whether they show at all) can be completely different.

Google is adamant that advertisers should submit the absolute most information for Sitelinks. In Examland we don't care why this is, only that it's their best practice is to go overboard on Sitelink information submitting.

All the URLs an advertiser submits as Sitelinks must be different pages of the same domain. *Clever Kevin* can't submit the same URLs with different titles, like repeatedly entering the URL of a single landing page but with a different link text each time. All URLs must share the same domain because the associated ad is only advertising one website.

Previous Visit Annotations

If a user's search triggers an ad for a site that she's been to before, then she could see a *Previous Visit Annotation* attached to the ad:

Portable Space Heaters
example.com/
Brand Names on Sale!
You visited three times. Last visit: 3 days ago.

Previous Visit Annotations rely on the user being logged-in to Google in order to work. Like Seller Ratings, these extensions are automatically applied and opting-out involves a form, so there won't be any questions about how to do either, though you might have to identify what the extension is for.

Review Extensions

You can post a favorable third party endorsement under your ad as a *Review Extension*. The blurb should be about the business as a whole and not any individual product or service and only one is eligible at a time. If you have dozens of great third-party quotes about your business, then pick the most persuasive one to appear:

Portable Space Heaters
example.com/
Brand Names on Sale!
"Absolutely the best place to buy brand names!" – Example Review Site

That "ding!" sound we just heard is the bell above *Clever Kevin's* head as it just struck him that he could fake a positive endorsement. All he has to do is throw-up a single page website called "Impartial Reviews of Places to Buy Brand Products" and then name himself as the winner of the world's greatest website contest and write himself a glowing review. Then he'll submit it as a Review Extension on his AdWords account. Brilliant.

Of course Googlers roll their eyes at this kind of misbehavior and these extensions have an extensive approval process. An exact or honestly paraphrased quote attributed and linked to a real published third party is eligible only after being verified by Google.

Review Extensions can be run at both the campaign and ad group level, but Google prefers you run them for whole campaigns and it prioritizes approval for those at the campaign level in order to create an artificial incentive for you do it that way.

Publishers aren't always willing to have their domains linked to for these purposes, so they can opt-out. The Search Exam isn't for publishers so (for the purpose of acing the test) you don't have to worry about the how this all looks from their perspective.

Newer Extensions & Annotations

Some ad extension types are still in beta testing or are still too new to be on the exam. *Communication Extensions* generate leads directly from an ad with no clickthrough necessary. *Image Extensions* enhance text ads with images. *Drop-Down Navigation Extensions* present users with a menu of sections of the advertised site, similar to Sitelinks. *Mobile App Extensions* (and *App Promotion Ads*) run on mobile devices only. Offer Extensions, Automatic Offer Extensions, Offer Ads, and Google Offers are constantly being reinvented and renamed.

Like other features, Google often makes new extensions available in stages. If any of these are ever finalized, it'll still be a while before they're available globally and even longer before they're on a certification exam. None of these gets its own chapter here because that won't help on the Search Exam.

CHAPTER 18: Analyzing Competition

The *Analyze Competition Tool* is not meant to analyze the competition so much as it's meant to analyze your own performance in light of theirs. Competitor performance data is aggregated and averaged so you won't be able to find out anything about the individual competitor you're most interested in and they won't be able to find out anything about you.

The Analyze Competition Tool can compare average position, clicks, clickthrough rate, or impressions. When you see how you stack up, first realize that you cannot be number one in every category because the way to rise in one is to fall in another. It's important to decide which metric matters the most and then pursue that one.

Categories & Sub-Categories

The Analyze Competition Tool divides all advertisers into about 7,000 sub-categories under about 50 categories. They're pretty sure we fit neatly into one (or a few) of them. Google says they're based on all the search queries that have ever triggered an ad and they're matched to us based on what the AdWords system finds in our landing pages, keywords, and ad copy.

Categories have sub-categories, which in turn have their own sub-categories – there are five levels in total, which is how they get to the number 7,000. Each sub-category that the tool lists for us is one that our ads have previously shown in and Google thinks we belong in.

To find out why we've been placed in a given sub-category (for the narrowest and lowest-level sub-category only) we can check the search terms that triggered our ads. It'll reveal what makes Google think we belong there. If they've got the wrong idea and have mis-categorized us, then Google assumes it's our fault for not appropriately using negative keywords and suggests we add more negatives to fix it.

Comparisons within Sub-Categories

Competition is analyzed by sub-category. Industries like travel, insurance, and for-profit education are notoriously competitive in search engine marketing. It's much tougher to rise in categories like those than others where advertisers put less time, effort, and money into optimizations. If your category is travel, then your comparisons are to other travel advertisers in the same sub-category and you are not being compared to those of other industries.

Google divides all advertisers that it thinks are in a sub-category into fifths and then tells you if you're in the top fifth, bottom fifth, or one of the fifths in between. This *Competitive Range* assessment is meant to encourage you to reach for the next highest fifth and it compliments those who most closely do everything Google's way by saying they're in the top fifth Competitive Range.

Detailed Comparisons are the narrowest of the Analyze Competition Tool's comparisons, not only restricting the comparison to only those in the same sub-category, but also to only those who are in the same Competitive Range within that sub-category. A travel advertiser in the bottom fifth, will only see a Detailed Comparison between them and others within that same bottom fifth of that same travel sub-category.

Auction Insights

There are often multiple and overlapping ways to get the information you're after and the *Auction Insights* report is so much like the Analyze Competition Tool that it's covered here instead of the upcoming chapter covering reports. The Auction Insights report can be run for campaigns, ad groups, or individual keywords and it shows Impression Share, Average Position, Overlap Rate, Position Above Rate, and Top of Page Percent. Those last three metrics aren't often cited so let's familiarize.

Overlap Rate shows how often you and others received impressions for the same keyword in the same auctions.

Position Above Rate should probably have been named the "Position Below Rate" because it shows how often your ad appeared below someone else's for the same keyword in the same auction.

Top of Page Rate shows how often your impressions for a keyword were at the top of the search results page (as opposed to the side or anywhere else).

Google uses the Auction Insights Report and the Analyze Competition Tool above to engender competition in a way that would be offensive if it weren't so helpful. There won't be any exam answer that relies on any Search Engine Intelligence tool not owned by Google or technique that could not be done completely within AdWords.

CHAPTER 19: Analyzing Performance

The two ways to analyze performance data are to view tables in the Campaigns Tab (the first half of this chapter) or to create reports (the second half).

Campaigns Tab

The *Campaigns Tab* should probably be called a "Performance Tab" because that's what it's all about. Inside are statistics by campaign, ad group, ad, and keyword. Under this tab there are seven sections that are also confusingly called "tabs."

Yes, the first tab within the Campaigns Tab is itself labeled "Campaigns." Imagine trying to describe this location: "First you open the Campaigns Tab and second you open the Campaigns Tab." It shows performance statistics by campaign.

The *Ad Groups Tab* shows ad group statistics, the *Ads Tab* shows them for individual ads, the *Keywords Tab* is for individual keywords, and the *Ad Extensions Tab* is naturally about ad extensions. The *Settings Tab* is just as appropriately named as those last few, with the distinction that it's only for settings at the campaign level. Those include a campaign's budget, bidding model, network(s), ad scheduling settings, language, location, and device settings.

The *Dimensions Tab* is no more important than any of the others, but we'll talk about it more than the others because it's not as intuitive. The Dimensions Tab lives under the Campaigns Tab just like the others we've just listed. It's where to get creative with the ways in which you'd like data presented to you. It also makes heavy use of labels which allow you to make any describable type of information pull-able into a report. Basically, we tell AdWords that we're interested in this one type of information and describe it in a way AdWords understands, then we start referring to this description as a *Label*. Whenever we want to see it again, we ask AdWords for it by that label.

We'll do this with an example client, Bram's Bikes. They run separate campaigns for mountain, road, BMX, fixed, cruiser, and recumbent bicycles and run separate campaigns which geographically target the Pacific, Southwest, and Rockies regions of the US. The same ads and keywords are running in three different geo-targeted campaigns. Bram can create the label *Road Bikes* and apply it to all road bike-related keywords and ads across his whole account. He can then use this label to filter for *Road Bike* keywords and see how they're doing across the account (no matter which campaign they're in) which allows him to compare how they're doing in the Rockies versus the Pacific.

The *Everything Else Row* shows everything that doesn't have a label. Google gives a great example of how this can be valuable (quoted from Google):

> *Since your branded keywords likely represent 10-20 keywords, you do not need to create a label for the thousands of non-branded keywords in your account. Rather, you can simply run a report on the branded label and see the results from the non-branded keywords reflected in the Everything Else row.*

The *Graph Option* exists to compare performance of a given metric across two time periods. It's possible to compare your CTR this July to CTR last July or your clicks from last week to clicks the week before last week. There are multiple graph options for seeing data from both time periods compared. They're limited to comparing only two time periods, so it can't graph three.

If you want to see multiple periods, then it's better to segment the data by time. You could create three *Segments* to compare each month of last quarter or thirty segments to compare each day of last month, or whatever else you find constructive. The results of this kind of analysis are what people who are not familiar with performance marketing expect to see in reports: A graph featuring an arrow-headed line that roller-coasters across days, months, or quarters..

This task can also be accomplished with the *Time View* in the Dimensions Tab. That makes three methods to compare time: the Graphs Option, Segments, and the Time View.

Reports

Reports are fully customizable in what goes in, what they do with it, and how it comes out. Reports can be viewed from within the AdWords dashboard, exported for use elsewhere, or they can arrive automatically by email. Just about anything can be used to start a report and you can generate one from any tab.

It's necessary to instruct AdWords in what you want a report about and how the resulting table should look when it's done. If you don't customize the table by specifying columns, segments, and filters, then you'll end up with more data than you want which hides the data you're interested in. There are some cookie-cutter *Preset Modules* that may already be what you want or be a good base to begin crafting a customized version. Commonly used preset modules are for things like keyword, ad, or destination URL performance. The rest of this chapter reviews a few report types.

Impression Share Report

We last visited *Ad Impression Share* (otherwise just called *Impression Share* (*IS*)) in an earlier chapter on Keyword Management. It's the number of impressions received divided by the number of impressions that could have been received. This "could have been received" number is based on eligibility, and determined by targeting settings, statuses, bids, and Quality Scores. An advertiser who narrows targeting settings is intentionally making his ads less eligible to show or one who raises bids is raising his ads' eligibility.

In un-Google-like fashion, Impression Share statistics are "only" updated daily, so the number you see today may actually be yesterday's statistic. There are both search and display Impression Share metrics. Only the search-related ones relevant to the Search Exam are listed here:

Search Impression Share is exactly what it sounds like, the IS from just google.com and the Search Network, excluding any Display Network figures.

Search Exact Match IS is written just like that and it's the Impression Share (for search only) for queries that were exact matches only.

Search Lost IS (Rank) is the percentage of ineligibility due to poor Ad Rank.

Search Lost IS (Budget) is the percentage of ineligibility due to insufficient budget. Because budgets are set at the campaign level, so is this metric.

Search Terms Report

Search terms and keywords are so closely related they're often thought of as the same thing. A *Search Term* is the user-generated query, it's what a user types into a search bar. A *Keyword* is the advertiser-generated word or words meant to connect their ads to users, it's what an advertiser is trying to be found for. In the case of an exact match they might be exactly the same, but in the case of other matches there's going to be a difference.

Advertisers are well aware of what their keywords are and can spend an inordinate amount of time building lists of them. If they want to know which search terms are actually leading people to their ads, then they're interested in the *Search Terms Report*. This is sometimes identified as *Keyword Details*, although Google seems uncomfortable with that term because whenever it appears in official literature it's in "quotation marks." The Search Terms Report (or "Keywords Details") shows which search terms lead users to the site, even if those terms are not already keywords. Their appearance here makes them good candidates to add as keywords. We last saw it mentioned in the chapter covering Dynamic Search Ads.

If a site were advertised with the phrase match keyword *quit smoking aides* and a user visited after searching for *buy quit smoking aides that work,* then we may choose to use that phrase as its own future exact match keyword. There may also be visits from people who searched for *quit smoking aids side effects.* The appearance of the phrase in the Search Terms Report may compel us to use the negative keyword *side effects* if that means the searcher is probably researching and not yet buying.

Sometimes a keyword that has been paused or deleted may still appear in our Search Terms Report. If the keyword *stop smoking aids* is paused, but the keyword *quit smoking aids* is active, then the active one might trigger an ad to be served on its paused variant (assuming *stop* is a variant of *quit*). A search term only shows in the report if it received at least one click in the last 30 days.

Geographic Reports

The *User Locations Report* only shows where users are physically located while the *Geographic Performance Report* shows both that and where users have shown interest. These reports have a lot of overlap with the earlier chapter on Location Extensions.

Let's repeat the differences between them in an example. Fulano's Cuenca del Plata Travel advertises Argentina travel packages to users who live in the United States. Their Geographic Performance Report might show much geographic targeting activity related to US cities and much related to Argentinian cities. That's because AdWords would serve some ads primarily because the user was interested in Argentina (maybe he searched the query *Argentina travel deals*) and other ads were served based more on the user's actual location (maybe a New Yorker just typed *travel deals*). AdWords is showing both of these location types in the same report.

But if Fulano's Travel just wants to compare the performance of their ads in different US cities, then they want to run a User Locations Report. It shows the actual locations where their ads were served, with no mention of the Argentinian locations that users were interested in.

Keyword Diagnosis Report

Keyword Diagnosis will reveal whether a keyword is triggering ads (or not) and its Quality Score. If a keyword isn't showing ads, then it'll show why and what to do about it. The *Keyword Diagnosis Panel* gives answers about specific types of visibility.

It's possible to check if ads are served on different domains, in different languages, different locations, and different device types. The answers it gives are only valid at the exact moment they're given, so the most recent diagnosis will be time-stamped.

Change History Report

If we have a team of people with access to our AdWords account, then the *Change History* report tracks who made which changes to the account and how these changes impacted performance. If an administrator is investigating some disastrous turn in an accounts statistics, then she can find out what changed and who changed it.

Change History also logs changes made via the AdWords Editor, AdWords API, and even Google's automated rules. It does *not* track adjustments made by the Budget Optimizer, or changes of ad statuses or passwords. It can take a few minutes for a change to post, so it's common to not see a change you made within the past few minutes reflected yet.

CHAPTER 20: Invalid Traffic

Google reassures us there's absolutely no reason to be concerned about invalid traffic. If you answer every question consistent with that idea, then you don't need to know anything else on the topic for the Search Exam. The test emphasizes those situations when traffic that could appear to be invalid is actually valid and it highlights Google's proactive measures to stop it, so we'll need some familiarity.

Valid Traffic is when real users with real intentions arrive on our site and *Invalid Traffic* is anything else. If Google thinks a visit doesn't represent real people or represents real people who aren't acting honestly, then they'll label that invalid traffic. *Invalid Clicks* are removed in real time before they accrue costs or sway statistics. *Invalid Impressions* are also filtered out and don't affect CTR or any other figure.

There are two ways to check on this data. You can see credit for it under the Billing Tab or you can include columns in reports for Invalid Clicks and Invalid Click Rates. These columns are turned off by default and opting-in doesn't create any new report, but includes the columns in regular reports.

No one (including Google) publically discloses all the techniques they use to detect invalid activity. AdWords examines every click for the obvious factors like IP address and timing, plus hundreds of others that they're not telling anyone about. This topic gets so much more complex than the laughably simplified examples you're about to read.

What's Invalid

All activity by any imaginable automated method is invalid. If an action is executed by a bot, spider, program (or whatever else) instead of a real finger on a mouse or touch screen, then it's invalid. But, that doesn't mean all real human traffic is valid.

Sometimes *Invalid Clicks* are everyday pedestrian happenings like a double-click. If a user double-clicks an ad, the advertiser pays for the first click and the second one goes into invalid traffic reporting. There's nothing automated about that and no malicious intent, just as click not worth paying for.

Now let's picture a town in which there are two pet shop owners, *Clever Kevin* and his competitive target, Harassed Hendrik. Both sell animals that didn't starve or freeze to death in the miserable puppy mills where pet shop puppies are bred. Harassed Hendrik advertises on AdWords with keywords like *cute fluffy puppy store.*

Clever Kevin instructs his son, *Clever Kevin junior*, to click Harassed Hendrik's ads 100 times a day in order to expend his advertising budget. Assuming Harassed Hendrik has an uncapped budget and pays hypothetical $1 CPCs, this could cost him $3,000 in a 30 day month if it worked. But it wouldn't work. AdWords would detect this activity and throw these human-generated (but invalid) clicks into invalid traffic reporting.

Maybe *Clever Kevin* begins advertising his own pet shop on AdWords too and hatches a plan to get a higher ad position than Harassed Hendrik. Instead of raising his own CTR, *Clever Kevin's* plan is to lower his competitor's. He instructs his son to search google.com 1,000 times a day for keywords that would trigger impressions of Harassed Hendrik's ads, but not their own ads. Junior doesn't click on any of them though. The goal is to trigger impressions but not click in order to artificially lower Harassed Hedrick's CTR, which would drag down Quality Score and ad position, leaving *Clever Kevin* at the top of the search results page. But this wouldn't work either. These *Invalid Impressions* are also detectable and also fall into the invalid traffic reporting.

Clever Kevin now puts his plans for Harassed Hendrik aside for a while to focus on his blog which defends the puppy mill industry. To monetize his site, he reserves space for AdWords to run ads and Google shares the revenue generated with him. Clever Kevin Junior notices that most of the ads that AdWords places on their blog are for canine protein supplements used for dog fighting. Junior asks his father "If Google pays us every time one of their ads on our website gets clicked, then why don't I just sit here and click ads on our own site all day?" Beaming with pride, *Clever Kevin* hasn't yet realized that AdWords would detect this activity too. The dog fighting suppliers whose ads Junior has fraudulently clicked will see his activity in their invalid traffic reporting.

Don't let these examples give you the idea that purposefully invalid traffic is typically the work of some misinformed knucklehead. In the real world these *Click Fraud* efforts are ridiculously complex, highly organized crime and this is the stuff that keeps Google engineers up at night. While only unethical advertisers commit click fraud, *all* advertisers are susceptible to it.

Google does not expect people like you and me who take AdWords exams to be experts on the subject, only that we answer exam questions in a way that shows we sleep soundly by trusting that Google is on top of it. They promise to cull the pack of bad actors and bad actions. Test questions will focus more on instances when advertisers mistake valid for invalid traffic which is where we turn next.

What's Valid

Advertisers who pay for a high volume of visits from users who don't convert might allege they were invalid. Google's first assumption when they stand accused is that our low conversion rate is more likely our fault and less likely theirs.

The reason could be our landing page isn't optimized for conversions. Or our competitors are getting better at PPC advertising, so users are more often choosing to buy from one of them. Maybe our keywords and ad copy aren't tightly-themed enough, so we've been giving users the wrong idea about what we offer. In any event, if the evidence that we're paying for invalid traffic is simply that our CTR has dropped, then Google says that alone is not enough to conclude anything is wrong.

Sometimes advertisers who see more than one click from the same IP address shout "Ah-Ha! I found invalid traffic!" Google's first response once again is that we probably have not. Return visits aren't considered invalid and Google insists we pay for them. A user who's comparison shopping different sites may click 20 ads (causing each advertiser to pay for a click). He may then decide he wants to see our site again, so to navigate his way back he types our site name into google.com to trigger our ad and clicks it for the second time today. Two clicks from one IP address, but nothing invalid about it.

Some users get their Internet service provided by *Internet Service Providers* who use a *Proxy IP* system in which all subscribers share the same IP address (most prevalent among the dial-up providers which still exist). Every subscriber to one of these services could appear in our logs with the same IP address so if we're visited by several of them then we'll see this valid activity in our statistics and pay for those ad clicks too.

While *Clever Kevin* is busy snickering at the idea of dial-up Internet, he's probably misunderstanding his web server logs. They include info from all visits, including Google's organic results. When they show repeat visits from the same user, that doesn't mean that we paid for these visits repeatedly because many could be referred by google.com's organic results.

Google's bots crawl all over the place and often trigger and then click on Google's own ads to see that everything is in proper working order. Google is well aware of what its own IP addresses are so there's no need to fear that they forgot about this and we're being charged for clicks that happen by their own system checks.

Google Instant

Then there's the peculiar case of somehow valid (yet arguably invalid) impressions delivered by Google Instant. When a user on google.com begins typing a search query, a drop-down list will present the queries that the system predicts the user might be in the process of typing. If a user has only had enough time to type the letter *u*, then Google might predict that they will type terms such as *utensils, upcoming,* or *ultimate.* In addition to the drop-down auto-suggest box, a full search results page can be generated with organic and paid results based on the prediction that the user is going to type *utensils.*

But if the next letter is *n,* it becomes clear that she's not typing *utensils, upcoming,* or *ultimate,* but something that starts with *un.* Now the auto-suggest box and search results page are updated with new predictions that start with *un,* like *unpainted, underwear,* and *unbreakable.* Next comes an *i,* so her term will begin with the letters *uni,* and the refreshed predictions now read *university, uniform,* and *unique.* You get the idea.

Google Instant seems to be under eternal development, so exactly what happens as someone types and how it's treated are changing. At the moment, valid ad impressions would count if the user clicks any suggestion or any result or pauses typing for three seconds. A user searching for the term *unique* could begin by typing the letter *u* and AdWords could predict the word *utensils,* which we will imagine is one of our keywords. If the user then pauses his typing for three seconds, then we have just had a valid non-clickthrough impression that AdWords would calculate into our statistics. This will affect our Impression Share, CTR, and other metrics.

When Invalid Goes Undetected

If the automatic filtering system misses some invalid traffic, then we're further assured the *Google Ad Traffic Quality Team* is constantly conducting *Proactive Analysis* to catch what the automated system misses. They won't say what that means, only that it's thorough.

If we think we've found invalid traffic that's otherwise gone undetected, the first thing Google wants us to do is review the click patterns over time to see if it can be explained by valid fluctuations in traffic.

It's possible that invalid traffic is discovered after the fact and has already been applied to our statistics and we've already paid a bill that included invalid clicks. When discovered, the traffic is removed from reports so as not to continue spoiling them and our account gets credited with the amount that had been paid for invalid activity. There's a two month statute of limitations on this so if it's not caught in two months, then it's not caught.

CHAPTER 21: Related Tools

Everything we've seen so far is executed in one place, the online AdWords dashboard that lives at adwords.google.com. There are two tools that each involve activity outside of that domain and we'll end the guide by covering both in this final chapter.

AdWords API

When logging-in to the AdWords dashboard, we're interfacing with AdWords data in a way that's useful to almost everybody. Everything we've studied about using AdWords has to do with interfacing with these data in this way. But let's say you have special needs and the AdWords dashboard that everyone else uses just won't cut it. If so, then you can design and run your own program which can intake the same info and then output whatever you want. Your very own client application program can interact with the same servers as the AdWords dashboard. In such a case you'd get and send data via the *AdWords API* (Application Programming Interface).

Most people who have any business getting an AdWords certification have no business diving deep into the world of APIs. The AdWords credentials suit people who have roles that involve things other than dealing with the AdWords API, which is typically programmers' territory. But there are exam questions about it. They're basic and simply assess whether you know what an API is, its benefits, and a little bit about the related developer token.

Marketers shouldn't be learning code or memorizing commands for the purposes of taking the test. Once you've passed it, the API-related sections of this chapter are what account managers and account executives are least likely to need to know outside of Examland. If you *are* a programmer, then this portion is focused only on the needs of the Search Exam and offers no actionable information.

The expense and headache of creating your own API-using program is justified if your own interface program could do something the AdWords dashboard and AdWords Editor cannot. Some programs integrate with our own inventory system to start and stop ads based on what's in stock or generate reports that incorporate data from other traffic sources like Bing, Facebook, or LinkedIn. An API can allow you to automate reporting and campaign management tasks, and make changes at scale. An advertiser with millions of keywords who needs to make frequent changes to bids would use the AdWords API as the best tool for the job.

The place to sign-up for the AdWords API is inside a *My Client Center* (MCC) account. Google will then assign a *Developer Token* (also called an *Authentication Token*) which is a unique text string that looks a lot like a product registration key. A fabricated token purely for illustration might look like this:

ABcdef123456-AB12_AB12.

The purpose of the token is to identify you to the API and allow the API to track who's accessing it. Every request your application sends must include the token in the *Request Header*.

One neat capability that can be executed via API is running simulations of campaigns to get an idea of how they would perform without running them live. The *Testing House* replaced the (now retired) *Programming Sandbox* but the term "Programming Sandbox" is still used on a test question which is still in circulation. Whatever you call it, this tool allows you to test new logic in your slick AdWords API-using application.

AdWords Editor

If we were going to build a general purpose application on the AdWords API, then we'd build something that looks a lot like the *AdWords Editor* (AE). It's a free downloadable desktop application for advertisers to manage their AdWords accounts. Every time someone sits down with AdWords Editor, he'll first download the current account, then make all the changes he wants, and finally upload those changes. That basic functionality (the ability to get work done while offline) is what the Editor can do (as an AdWords API application) that the online dashboard can't.

Changes can be to add, edit, delete, copy or move campaigns, ad groups, ads, or keywords. Large-scale bulk changes and advanced searches can be done more quickly through AdWords Editor, especially across multiple accounts. It can also be used to back-up AdWords accounts for archiving or sharing.

Only one account can be edited at any given time, but it's not too difficult to switch between them or make sweeping changes to an MCC which affect all accounts within that MCC.

If you've been using AdWords Editor in the real world, check for an updated version just in case there are new features that pop-up on the Search Exam. You would only know what they are by having the freshest version installed.

We can search for keywords with a high or low CTR, average positions, clicks, or other attributes. Maybe we want to see all keywords with an average position of 10 or higher, but zero clicks. Or maybe we need to search for all keywords with an average position of at least three, but a CTR of less than 1%. All of the suggestions that have been seen on how to use search have to do with either searching for keywords to pause or searching for keywords to raise bids on.

AdWords Editor has a few novel keyword tools that we'll just list here. There's a lot of overlapping functionality between them and there's also overlap with the functions of the Keyword Planner so selecting the "best" tool for a given task is personal preference. That kind of subjectivity means the exam won't ask you which one is right, but you should be aware of what each one does.

Keyword Grouper automatically re-sorts an existing keyword list into new ad groups that Google thinks are tightly themed, or "grouped."

Keyword Multiplier combines a list of adjectives with a list of nouns to generate a list of potential new keywords

Keyword Expansion Tool generates a list of potential new keywords sourced from a base keyword that you'd enter to begin the process.

Search-Based Keywords Tool generates a list of user queries which Google thinks are related to your website's URL.

The first step when beginning a workday in AdWords Editor is to ensure the most recent version of campaign information is currently downloaded. This is vitally important when there are several people working on the same account, because much effort could be wasted optimizing old information. The first thing someone who logs-in to a shared AdWords Editor account should do is click *Get Recent Changes* in the tool bar.

The "get recent changes refresh" can be done with the *Basic Option* or the *More Data Option*. The Basic Option is faster but pulls less information. The More Data Option is slower, but includes more data such as Top of Page and First Page Bid Estimates, Quality Scores, and the current ad approval statuses.

A comment can be attached to anything in the AdWords Editor. Comments are used by the commenter as personal reminders, or to explain something when an account is shared with others. Users can also circulate potential changes for comment before actually posting them. AE keeps its own Change History data which tracks which person made which changes. It's similar to AdWords' own Change History report mentioned earlier.

The *Check Changes* feature reviews unposted changes for compliance with AdWords policies. Once imported into AdWords, changes that were made in AdWords Editor will take effect right away. But, we're cautioned that there "may be a slight delay" before all changes take full effect.

At the end of a session with the AE, once you're at a stopping point and everything looks in order, it's necessary to post the changes. This is the moment when whatever you did in the editor goes live in the associated AdWords account. Any change in AE that has not been posted can be *Reverted* (undone). This is a sweeping feature that affects all unposted changes, so it's not a "back button" or "undo button" but an "erase all unposted changes at the same time" button. Once posted, the changes are live on live traffic.

Some issues cannot be changed in AdWords Editor. These range from whole-account issues like bidding options and account-level billing preferences to low-level issues like ad-level Location Extensions. Anything that can't be done in AdWords Editor can be done in AdWords, so the solution to any capability issue with AE is to log directly in to the AdWords dashboard online.

NOW WHAT?

Humor Google's hubris. In Examland, it's understood that everything Google does is best done by Google, every product they offer is the best, and their best practices are *the only* best practices. Good luck on your Exam! I invite you to contact me after it's all said and done.

So, now what?

Rate: Has this guide helped you? Please give it 5 stars on Amazon.com! I publish this guide independently, so a great review means everything.

Respond: Tell me how to make this guide better: Keith@KeithPenn.com

Practice: The best exam practice questions are on iPassExam. Get current discount codes at KeithPenn.com/discounts.

Prepare: This guide covers one AdWords Exam. There are others.

Connect:

Updated Info: SearchCerts.com

Author site: KeithPenn.com

Follow on Twitter: @SearchCerts

Circle on Google+: Plus.Google.com/+KeithPenn

Connect on LinkedIn: LinkedIn.com/in/KeithPenn